DARK FEMININE ENERGY

BECOME A FEMME FATALE THROUGH SELF-DISCOVERY, UNEARTHING DARK FEMININE SECRETS, AND MASTERING THE ART OF SEDUCTION WITH SELF-CONFIDENCE.

NORA HAZE

Dark Feminine Energy

© Copyright 2023 Nora Haze All rights reserved.

Written by Nora Haze

First Edition

TABLE OF CONTENTS

INTRODUCTION   9
Unveiling the Magnetic Pull of Your Inner
Femme Fatale   9
Unlocking the Mystique of "Dark Feminine
Energy"   10
A Guide to Using This Book: Your Roadmap to
Femme Fatale Fabulousness   12

CHAPTER 1   17
What is Dark Feminine Energy?   17
The Historical Perspective   19
The Yin and Yang: Balancing Light and Dark   22
The Science of Energy; Dark Matter and Dark
Femininity   24

CHAPTER 2   27
The Allure of the Femme Fatale   27
Mastering the Look; Femme Fatale Fashion   31
Femme Fatale Behavior and Mannerisms   34
Crafting Your Femme Fatale Narrative   38
Building Your Femme Fatale Skill Set   40

CHAPTER 3   43
The Psychology Behind the Secrets   43
Guarding Your Mystique   45
The Art of Being Unpredictable   48
Why Keeping Secrets Enhances Your Dark
Energy   49

CHAPTER 4   52
Inner Confidence vs. Outer Show   52
Self-Acceptance: Loving the Dark and Light   54
Strategies for Building Lasting Confidence   55
Overcoming Insecurities with Dark Energy   56

CHAPTER 5   59
How to Seduce Any Man   59
The Five Phases of Seduction   61
Mind Games and the Power of Suggestion   62
Sexual Chemistry and Dark Feminine Energy   64
Mastering the Art of Seduction   66

CHAPTER 6   68
Power in Relationships: An Overview   68
Leveraging Your Dark Feminine Energy at Work   72
Conflict Resolution; The Dark Feminine Way   74

CHAPTER 7   77
The Dark Goddess. Archetypes and Myth
Unveiling the Cosmic Blueprint   77
Spiritual Practices for Harnessing Your Dark
Energy. Your Cosmic Toolkit for Unearthly
Allure   79
The Empowering Influence of Shadow Work;
Transmuting Your Darkness, into Valuable
Lessons   81
Astrology and the Dark Feminine; How the Stars
Shape Your Inner Femme Fatale   83
The Intersection of Feminism and Dark
Femininity Where Empowerment Meets Allure   85

CHAPTER 8   88
Embracing Your Full Self - The Risks and
Rewards of Living on the Boundaries, between
Lightness and Darkness   88
Crafting Your Brand of Dainty - Designing Your
Femme Fatale Persona from Scratch   90
Embracing Your Truest Self and Unleashing
Your Potential   92
Creating a Life That Honors Your Dark Energy;
Your Blueprint for a Life That's as Enigmatic as
You Are   94

Conclusion   97

Acknowledgments   101

INTRODUCTION

UNVEILING THE MAGNETIC PULL OF YOUR INNER FEMME FATALE

*Y*es, I'm addressing you—the captivating woman holding this book now. Firstly, give yourself a pat on the back, for picking up this book. Why? Because you're about to embark on a journey of self-discovery, empowerment, and embracing your femininity without any apologies. Trust me; it's going to be a life-changing and incredibly enjoyable experience!

Have you ever come across the concept of Dark Feminine Energy? If not get ready for an adventure, my queen! This isn't your guide on being the " girl" who always ends up last. No way! Instead, consider this as your pass into the realm of the Femme Fatale—a place where mystery intertwines with mastery and where seduction becomes your nature.

I can anticipate what's probably crossing your mind now. "Dark Feminine Energy? Sounds like something related to witchcraft or taboo topics." Well, let me assure you—how mistaken that assumption is! The term "dark" here doesn't imply evil; rather it signifies being unrestrained, authentic, and yourself. It represents that side of you that remains enigmatic yet alluringly irresistible—the side that perhaps you've hidden away until now due to concerns, about others' opinions.

Are you ready for an adventure, my dear? We will delve into the depths of understanding the energy that surrounds us. Uncover the secrets of being a Femme Fatale, which can help you captivate any man or simply make life more intriguing. We'll also explore how to harness this energy in your work relationships and even find your community.

What should you expect? Think of this as your treasure trove of Dark Feminine secrets revealed and explained with a hint of intrigue. We'll dive into history, psychology offers fashion tips galore discuss power dynamics, and touch on spirituality. If ever there was a guide to becoming a modern-day Cleopatra this is it!

Are you tired of playing small? Do you yearn to embrace your power and allure effortlessly? Then let's not waste another moment. Turn that page and embark on a journey to unleash the captivating version of yourself.

Ready? Set. Embrace your Femme Fatale!

UNLOCKING THE MYSTIQUE OF "DARK FEMININE ENERGY"

Ah! You've turned the page! See? You're already one step closer, to unlocking that mesmerizing aura within you.

So, let's dive into the essence of this Dark Feminine Energy that we've been discussing much. If I had to sum it up in one word? Enchantment. No, I don't mean pulling rabbits out of hats or casting spells (although who's to say you can't?). I'm referring to a kind of enchantment that radiates from, within when you're completely attuned to every aspect of yourself. The light, the dark, and all those beautiful shades in between.

Just imagine stepping into a room and feeling like you own it. Not because you're the loudest or the extroverted person present. Because your energy is so captivating people can't help but be drawn towards you. This energy is ancient, almost primal yet perfectly relevant in today's world. It has been the hidden force behind sirens, sorceresses, and influential women throughout history. From Cleopatra to Marilyn Monroe this energy has shaped destinies. Even brought down empires... Guess what? You possess it within yourself well.

". How do I tap into it?" Ahh, I'm glad you asked! First things first; let's debunk a misconception. Dark Feminine Energy isn't about manipulation or deceit. It's not, about being a 'bad girl' either.

Instead, it's embracing every aspect of your femininity—the mysterious and the clear—without being afraid of society's judgments. Imagine yourself as a diamond with facets that dazzle. Never revealing everything all at once. You have the power to choose what to show when to show it and to whom. The real allure lies in this ability to make choices and, in the possibilities you represent.

We will explore techniques that can help you nurture this energy from your fashion choices (yes fashion is not just frivolous; it serves as both armor and a statement) to your behaviors and even the psychology behind keeping well-kept secrets.

By the end of this section the idea of "Dark Feminine Energy" won't just be a concept; it will become a part of your lived experience... Let me assure you it will add intrigue to your life —whether you're negotiating business deals captivating someone romantically or simply enjoying your irresistibly mysterious company.

Are you ready to unlock the treasure trove of your mystique? The key is already, in your hands—this book—and importantly your willingness to dive into the depths of the unknown that are dark yet delightfully enchanting.

A GUIDE TO USING THIS BOOK: YOUR ROADMAP TO FEMME FATALE FABULOUSNESS

Welcome, my friend! I can sense your excitement. I'm here to guide you on your journey, towards embracing your femme fatale allure... First, let's talk logistics before diving into the captivating world of Dark Feminine Energy. All embarking on an adventure without a roadmap would be quite risky don't you think?

Now I must emphasize the importance of taking things slow and savoring this experience. I know that your inner femme fatale is eager to conquer the world in a flash but trust me, darling immersing yourself fully in this journey will make reaching your destination more rewarding.

Let's delve into how this book is structured. It's divided into sections that explore aspects of your enchanting persona.

Chapter 1: Understanding Dark Feminine Energy - Laying Your Foundation

Consider this section as Femme Fatale 101. Just as you wouldn't step onto a dance floor without knowing the steps we'll delve into what Dark Feminine Energy is all, about. We'll explore its roots. Dive into the timeless concept of balancing yin and yang. Mastering these elements will set the stage for all the moves that lie ahead.

Chapter 2: Becoming a Femme Fatale - Get Ready for Something Amazing!

Are you ready to take it up a notch? In this section, we're going out. From your fashion choices to your demeanor, this is your transformation kit. Think of it as having your personal style advisor, life mentor, and confidence booster all wrapped up in one package. It's going to be an experience!

Chapter 3: Dark Feminine Secrets - Our Little Secret!

Come closer this part is between us alright? We're delving into the depths of your aura. Discover how to keep others guessing, embrace unpredictability, and understand why a touch of secrecy can be your ally... Remember, these are not tricks; they are integral components of your multi-faceted personality. So, let's keep it exclusive... Shh!

Chapter 4: Boosting Your Confidence - Flaunt Your Radiance, with Pride!

Being a Femme Fatale requires unwavering self-assurance. In this segment, we'll address the element of confidence (the big C). Discover the strength and exude poise outwardly. Learn actionable strategies to maintain high energy levels in any situation.

Afterward, you'll enter any room with confidence and poise (because let's be honest you will).

Chapter 5: Seduction and Relationships - Prepare to Make an Impression!

Whether you're single dating or in a relationship this section delves into the dynamics that make you irresistible. We'll discuss not only seduction but also how to captivate and engage anyone who crosses your path.

Chapter 6: Power Dynamics and Manipulation - Proceed with Caution!

It's not all fun and games; having power also brings responsibility. Learn how to navigate dynamics, like a pro, both in your personal life and professional endeavors... Always remember to use your influence for good purposes!

Chapter 7: Making Spiritual Connections and Growing Personally

It's not, about looking the part; it's about embodying it. We delve into archetypes, myths, and how to tap into your energy for growth. This section explores the concept of the "Dark Goddess". How you can harness your power effectively.

Chapter 8: Embracing Authenticity

Prepare yourself to confront some truths because we're discussing embracing yourself. Here you'll learn to integrate your Femme Fatale persona with your life and genuinely live in alignment, with who you are.

The Skill of Selectivity

Listen not every aspect of this book will resonate with you. That's perfectly alright. We all possess our versions of allure. So, feel free to skip around chapters or delve into sections that truly speak to you. However, keep in mind that the more effort you invest in this journey the greater the rewards will be. It's all about your commitment, my dear.

We've put a lot of consideration into the length of each chapter and it's not random—we genuinely have your interests, in mind! Here's why;

Tailored for Easy Reading

Every chapter has been carefully crafted to provide a self-contained source of wisdom. Think of it as a taste of feminine knowledge that you can enjoy and absorb effortlessly. It offers enough to reflect upon as you navigate through your wonderful day.

Keeps You Engaged

We've fine-tuned the chapters to keep you captivated. Say goodbye to thinking "I'll read it later". Hello to wondering "What comes next?" You'll find yourself naturally transitioning from one chapter to another with each one drawing you into your journey toward embracing your Femme Fatale.

Opportunities for Contemplation

The unique length allows space for the wisdom to sink in. It's about giving yourself time to absorb contemplate and incorporate these transformative insights into your life. Let each chapter linger in your thoughts; you'll be amazed by how it resonates with you.

Adaptable to Your Lifestyle

Whether you're grabbing a coffee or waiting for a friend each chapter perfectly fits those moments in, between that life throws at us. Take it with you wherever you go ensuring that you never miss out on empowering yourself along the way.

Created for Your Satisfaction

Every chapter provides a self-contained dose of wisdom allowing you to savor the feeling of accomplishment. Finishing each one is akin, to discovering gems of empowerment and who wouldn't enjoy embarking on a treasure hunt?

Customized Just for You

Craving something spiritual? Maybe you're in the mood, for an approach? Each chapter stands independently presenting an array of Femme Fatale essentials that cater to your mood or requirement.

Are you prepared to utilize this guide and embrace your Femme Fatale? Let us begin our journey and discover everything that makes you uniquely and unapologetically yourself.

CHAPTER 1

UNDERSTANDING DARK FEMININE ENERGY

WHAT IS DARK FEMININE ENERGY?

*U*nleashing Your Inner Strength

Picture this; You enter a room and immediately sense a shift, in the atmosphere. Heads turn, eyes meet, and suddenly there's an energy in the air. It's as if you've cast a spell captivating both men and women alike with a force. But this power isn't some trick or magical potion—it's something potent that has always resided within you; your dark feminine energy.

So, what is this enigmatic force? Is it a subject that's whispered about but rarely discussed openly? Is it a power waiting to be embraced by those who are courageous enough to explore the depths of their souls?

Let's set one thing straight; Dark feminine energy is not inherently evil or malicious. Contrary, to belief it has nothing to do with manipulation or causing harm. These misconceptions have been perpetuated by age narratives designed to suppress and undermine the power of femininity.

In a world that has long valued traits such, as logic, aggression and stoicism traditionally associated with masculinity the intuitive nature of feminine energy has unfortunately been overlooked and even stigmatized.

Are you intrigued? Then continue reading.

Dark feminine energy serves as a complement to the recognized qualities of light feminine energy. While light feminine energy embodies nurturing, compassion, and openness the dark feminine is characterized by introspection, intuition, and unapologetic intensity.

Consider them as two sides of the coin; they cannot exist independently. Just like Yin needs Yang to balance your complete spectrum of energy from light to dark requires harmonization for you to be true, to yourself.

Let's take a moment to ponder the moon—a symbol of femininity. Like its side that reflects sunlight, it also possesses a mysterious dark side. This darkness doesn't lack power; instead, it exerts a pull that affects our planet's tides. Similarly, your feminine energy holds influence—often more potent because it operates beneath the surface unseen but deeply felt.

Still not convinced? Brace yourself for what comes!

This is where things become truly captivating.

When you embrace the depths of your energy you unlock a range of emotional and even sexual capabilities that society has conditioned you to suppress. The art of allure the excitement of unpredictability and the ability to form spiritual connections can all become accessible to you. Imagine being in tune, with your world so that your intuition becomes incredibly sharp guiding you through relationships, work situations, and personal challenges.

However, it is important to handle this power with care. Dark feminine energy should not be treated as a plaything. If left uncontrolled it can lead to behavior patterns, toxic relationships, and an imbalanced life. That's why this book goes beyond being a revelation; it is also a responsibility.

As you peruse these pages you are not simply learning about energy; rather you are discovering how to wield it wisely while maintaining dignity and true strength.

So, if there have been moments when you sensed that there is more version of yourself waiting to be unleashed.

Know that your intuition is correct. Whether you are already connected with your side or find yourself standing at its threshold with curiosity yet hesitation this book extends an invitation for you to fully embrace your power.

Let's start your transformation now. Why settle for a life where you only give half of your potential when you have the power to unlock your capabilities at your fingertips?

THE HISTORICAL PERSPECTIVE

From Witch Hunts to Hollywood; Revealing the Enigmatic Feminine Throughout Different Eras

Imagine this; It's a moonlit night back in the Middle Ages. In a village, there is a woman who is respected for her wisdom and healing abilities.

She gathers herbs for her remedies when suddenly she is seized, accused of practicing witchcraft, and ultimately burned at the stake. What was her crime? She dared to tap into an energy that her society couldn't comprehend or control.

What they labeled as 'witchcraft' was essentially an expression of what we recognize as dark feminine energy.

Fast forward a few centuries. We encounter the emergence of the 'Femme Fatale' in literature and movies captivating our imaginations.

From Cleopatra's danger to Marlene Dietrich's charm, on screen, dark feminine energy persists but often remains associated with villainy or temptation.

What connects these episodes? Let's delve deeper.

Throughout history, people have been captivated by frightened of, and sometimes actively persecuted those who possess energy... Why? Because it challenges the standing norms that have always prioritized masculine energy while relegating feminine energy, especially its darker aspects to the outskirts of acceptability.

An Edged Sword; Empowerment and Vilification.

In civilizations goddesses, like Kali in Hinduism and Hecate in mythology were once highly revered for embodying traits such as wisdom, strength, and even destruction. Acknowledging the immense power that feminine energy could possess.

However, with the rise of societies, these figures were. Pushed to the margins of society. Their stories were rewritten to fit narratives that aimed to restrict femininity within more "acceptable" boundaries.

Why is it important for you to be aware of this history? Let me explain.

Understanding the context becomes crucial for those who desire to powerfully embrace their dark feminine energy today. By knowing where we come from we gain insight into where we need to go. It also helps us recognize why you might have hesitated to embrace your dark feminine energy due to society's often negative perceptions.

Subtle yet Significant; The Modern Revival.

Although times have. Witch hunts are no longer prevalent echoes of these attitudes still linger, in modern society. Nevertheless, something fascinating is unfolding before our eyes.

More and more women are embracing their feminine energy incorporating it into a new concept of feminine power. Celebrities, politicians, and everyday women alike are finding a balance, between the dark aspects of their femininity resulting in a genuine and impactful presence.

Don't overlook the growing movement.

There is a wave of change happening. You don't want to miss out. Women are discovering ways to harness the power of their energy in various areas of life from the workplace to personal relationships. By integrating this side of themselves they are breaking barriers and challenging stereotypes. Redefining what it means to be a woman in today's world.

The past sets the stage for your future.

Throughout history feminine energy has been both. Condemned —a complex tapestry of contradictions... In every era, there have been individuals enough to embrace this mysterious force and leave an enduring impact on society and culture. As you explore the pages of this book remember that you are not just studying history; you are a participant, in shaping the narrative of feminine energy for generations to come.

Are you ready to embrace your spectrum and be a part of history? Your journey continues here with the captivating stories and hidden truths waiting to be revealed in the chapters. Get ready, for an exhilarating update to your perspective.

THE YIN AND YANG: BALANCING LIGHT AND DARK

Discovering the Divine Harmony of Opposites

Picture this; You're standing at the edge of the ocean watching as the sun gracefully disappears below the horizon. In that moment of twilight, you witness a mesmerizing dance between opposites.

Oranges contrast with cool blues a setting sun meeting a rising moon and the rhythmic ebb and flow of tides. This enchanting interplay is what Yin and Yang symbolize. A philosophy that beautifully captures the essence of opposing forces... How does it relate to your exploration into the depths of feminine energy?

Hold on tight because this might just be the revelation you've been waiting for.

Things Yin and Yang aren't about good versus evil; it's all, about finding balance and harmony through embracing different energies that together form a complete whole.

When we talk about energy we can think of light, as Yin. Dark as Yang. Yin represents nurturing, empathy, and openness while Yang embodies potency, mystery, and introspection. It might seem confusing or intriguing at first. Let's connect the dots.

Understanding the concept of Yin and Yang gives us a framework to embrace our feminine energy while staying connected to our light side. It's about finding a balance that allows us to be our most authentic and empowered selves. Imagine the freedom of living without being confined by expectations that try to label us in one category or another.

There's more depth to this ancient philosophy than meets the eye. The theory of Yin and Yang teaches us that each force contains a hint of its opposite within it.

If you look at the symbol closely, you'll notice a dot in the white swirl and vice versa. What does this mean for you? In your nurturing moments, there is a touch of assertive darkness, within you.

Similarly, when you're fully embracing your femme fatale side there is still a current of energy present.

Why is this duality so important? Stay with me; we're about to delve into it.

True magic occurs when you learn to switch between these energies adapting your approach to situations. Picture yourself negotiating a business deal with the combination of assertiveness and empathy or navigating a relationship that is both exciting and deeply emotional. That's the power of comprehending and applying the Yin and Yang in your life.

Don't overlook the revolution happening within.

And here's an interesting twist; this isn't some concept; it's a way of life. The women who truly grasp the balance, between light and dark, are the ones making an impact. They are the entrepreneurs, influencers, thought leaders, and passionate rebels who refuse to conform to society's expectations... You know what? They're also the happiest because they have achieved a level of self-acceptance that most people can only dream about.

Caution: This will transform you.

Integrating the wisdom of Yin and Yang into your understanding of energy is not merely an exercise; it brings about profound change. It involves rewriting the narrative overturning centuries of paradigms that have restricted and limited women. By attaining this equilibrium you're not just breaking free from constraints; you're establishing a standard, for feminine empowerment.

Are you prepared to embrace a future where your energy is, in balance? Are you ready to join the women who have found tranquility by harmonizing the Yin and Yang within themselves? Your response to these queries will not shape the quality of your life. Also, determine your ability to impact and revolutionize the world around you. This is more than another chapter in a book; it's a moment, in your life narrative. Turn the page. Let the journey commence.

THE SCIENCE OF ENERGY; DARK MATTER AND DARK FEMININITY

Blurring Boundaries; The Intersection of Science and Spirituality

Imagine this; You find yourself floating amidst the expanse of the cosmos surrounded by bodies, shimmering galaxies, and the captivating allure of the unknown. What may escape your awareness is that this awe-inspiring spectacle is predominantly composed of something matter—a phenomenon that cannot be seen touched or easily comprehended. Similar, to the enigmatic yet present concept of feminine energy dark matter remains an unsolved puzzle that binds our universe together.

Get ready for an exhilarating journey as we delve deeper into this subject.

Dark matter comprises 27% of our universe; however, its detection remains elusive. Like energy, it exerts a powerful but invisible force that influences the movements and behaviors of everything around it. While scientists grapple with unraveling the nature of matter women worldwide are awakening to their own potent yet mysterious reservoirs of dark feminine energy.

Intrigued? You should be. Let's explore why all this holds significance.

To fully comprehend and embrace your capacity, for feminine energy, it is essential to approach it from various perspectives — including a scientific one.

Understanding the connections, between matter and the concept of feminine energy adds a new layer of depth to your journey. It's like using a microscope to gain insights into what drives you and everything starts making sense in a whole new way.

Let's Move Beyond Spiritual Concepts and Embrace Scientific Perspectives.

I can anticipate your thoughts; "Isn't this more of an idea?" Absolutely, but that doesn't mean we can't enrich it with understanding. When science and spirituality come together it creates a fusion that empowers you to explore your feminine energy with both logic and emotion.

Stay with me as We Venture into Unexplored Territory.

While there is no study linking dark matter to dark feminine energy there are metaphorical similarities that are too intriguing to disregard. Both are elusive aspects of existence; they have an influence on everything around them but have often been misunderstood or undervalued throughout history.

Are You Ready for a Reality Check?

If you genuinely want to grasp and harness the power of your energy, it's vital not to overlook its multifaceted nature. Like a gemstone, with facets and angles, your dark energy is intricate calling for an approach to truly comprehend it.

Don't settle for a perspective; embrace complexity and thrive on it as a woman. Connect with the universe. Recognize that you are a part of it.

When you start seeing your energy as a natural force, similar, to dark matter in science it deepens your understanding and acceptance of this powerful characteristic. It enables you to move beyond judgments and self-imposed limitations. You're not an anomaly; you're a phenomenon an interplay of energies that shape the world around you.

The key takeaway is that your dark energy is a phenomenon. So, as you continue reading this book remember that you're not simply diving into myths or psychological theories. You're tapping into a force as the dark matter holds galaxies together. Yes, like stars, universes, and the infinite cosmos – you are made of the essence. Let that sink in.

Now comes the exciting part; Are you ready to explore? This journey isn't about growth or individual power; it's, about aligning yourself with the cosmic order. By doing you unlock levels of understanding that go beyond what appears in your reflection every day.

You're tapping into a connection, with the universe that most people never even consider, let alone experience. So, take a moment to appreciate the vastness of what lies.

Now are you prepared to become a presence? Your journey into the realms of energy and science starts now.

CHAPTER 2

BECOMING A FEMME FATALE

THE ALLURE OF THE FEMME FATALE

Unveiling the Enigma; The Captivating Force You Can't Resist

Picture this; You enter a room. Immediately sense an energy that envelops the space – a magnetic force that attracts all eyes toward one direction. At the core of this field stands a woman. She may not be the flamboyant person in the room, but she exudes confidence and commands attention. She possesses an air of mystery so enigmatic that you cannot help but be drawn in. Welcome to the world of women.

Grab your glass of wine or cup of herbal tea; we are about to unravel the secrets behind one of history's most enduring archetypes.

What Makes Her So Irresistibly Alluring?

First things first; What is it, about women that makes them irresistibly captivating? Is it their beauty? No, because we all understand that beauty is a concept. Is it her intelligence? Maybe, but that's not the story. It's her aura, her captivating aura that distinguishes her from the rest. It's a captivating combination of mystery, sensuality, and strength that she skillfully wields.

Wait; brace yourself for an experience that could challenge everything you thought you knew about allure.

The Femme Fatale, in History and Culture Let's take a moment to acknowledge the Femme Fatale figures who have left their mark on history and pop culture; Cleopatra, Mata Hari, and fictional characters like Cat Woman and Jessica Rabbit. These women share more than their charm; they embody a type of femininity that defies societal norms pushing boundaries and surpassing expectations.

Intrigued? This isn't about them; this is about discovering the Femme Fatale within yourself.

Beauty, vs. Energy; The True Source of Attraction

Many people believe that the appeal of a Femme Fatale primarily stems from her beauty. Let's debunk that misconception. While physical attractiveness may play a role the true allure lies in her energy how she carries herself the sense of intrigue surrounding her and the subtle, yet impactful messages conveyed by her presence. It's your chance to redefine the norms; True beauty isn't, about what you possess; it's about the radiance you emanate.

Exploring Emotional Depths; From Vulnerability to Empowerment

Now things become truly fascinating. The Femme Fatale is not a one character; she embodies a complex fusion of vulnerability and strength, gentleness and power. She can be as delicate as a petal. As fierce as a lioness within the same breath. It's this range of emotions that makes her so captivating and multi-faceted.

And here's the best part; this emotional spectrum is not limited to a chosen few; it is accessible to each one of us.

Challenging Social Conventions; The Femme Fatales Relationship, with Society

In our world women are often boxed into stereotypes that are constraining and myopic. However, the Femme Fatale defies these expectations by refusing to conform. She breaks rules sets trends and above all else she is a spirit who charts her path.

Imagine if I were to tell you that breaking the rules isn't just reserved for rebels. It's something that anyone ready to live life on their terms can do.

The Femme Fatale and her Connection, to Dark Feminine Energy; A Match Made in Heaven

This is where the magic happens; the Femme Fatale archetype represents the embodiment of energy. She encapsulates the essence of mystery, sensuality, and primal strength that arises from embracing this captivating force. She isn't merely a character; she is a living breathing testament to the power of the feminine.

Feeling a connection? You should because this is about uncovering the potential that resides within you.

Embracing Your Femme Fatale Energy

How does one tap into this Femme Fatale energy? It all starts with self-awareness. Embracing your dark feminine qualities. It involves letting go of norms and aligning with yourself... Above all, it means utilizing this energy as a means of empowerment rather, than manipulation.

Pay attention; Once you master this you're not only transforming your life but also reshaping narratives for women everywhere.

The Duality of Risks and Rewards; Exploring the Femme Fatale Energy

like anything that possesses potency and power the energy of a Femme Fatale brings both risks and rewards. The risk lies in mishandling this energy and becoming a caricature of an empowered woman. On the other hand, the reward is living life on your terms exuding an irresistible charm that stems from inner strength rather, than desperation.

Pause for a moment to contemplate this notion; With great power comes responsibility. Are you prepared to handle it?

Embracing the Future as a Femme Fatale

So where does this leave us? It leaves us with possibilities. As women increasingly embrace their energy, we are likely to witness more instances of Femme Fatales emerging not only in stories and legends but also in everyday reality—women who fearlessly embrace their power feel empowered and unapologetically express themselves.

But here's the climax; This future isn't about them; it's about you too. You can embody the essence of a Femme Fatale—a source of feminine energy illuminating paths, for others.

MASTERING THE LOOK; FEMME FATALE FASHION

The Foundation; Beyond Mere Clothing Let's set things from the beginning; Fashion is more than vanity or superficiality; it serves as a vital means of self-expression. For the Femme Fatale, her wardrobe goes beyond a collection of garments; it acts as an arsenal of tools to communicate her identity. In a world where first impressions often leave a lasting impact mastering your appearance becomes the step towards unleashing your Femme Fatale.

In essence, your fashion choices go beyond aesthetics; they hold significance.

Beyond the Classic Black Dress; The Palette of a Femme Fatale

While black tends to dominate the wardrobe of a Femme Fatale she isn't limited to one style. Deep reds, rich purples, and metallic hues can all contribute to capturing the essence of that energy you seek. The key lies in selecting colors that resonate with your aura rather than solely following trends.

Your color palette acts as your language; ensure it narrates the tale.

Decoding Textures; Silk, Lace, and Leather

Much like colors the choice of fabrics adds texture and dimension, to your look. Imagine the feel of silks flowing like water the intricate beauty of delicate yet strong lace or the empowering aura of rugged leather. Each fabric expresses a facet of your feminine energy.

So, what's your texture? The fabrics you select go beyond being materials; they possess their tactile language.

To. Not to accessorize? That's not the question! The true question is how to accessorize. Consider statement jewelry ornate hairpins or even a classic red lip. Each accessory should be a choice that enhances your look and adds depth. It's all, about the details that can subtly convey messages about your identity and values.

Your mission? Select accessories that infuse a touch of drama without overshadowing your essence.

Let's not forget about shoes – those heroes. Stilettos boots, sneakers... Each footwear option makes its statement. But what truly matters is how you carry yourself while wearing them – it can turn wearing a pair into embodying them

The moral of this story? Your choice of fabrics, accessories, and shoes is an opportunity to express yourself authentically and empower your energy.

Never underestimate the power that a killer pair of shoes holds.

Femme Fatale Hairstyles; A Captivating Beauty

Whether you opt for waves a daring pixie cut or cascading extensions, down your back your hairstyle speaks volumes about your identity. It's essential to consider the message you wish to convey. Are you embracing the timeless grace of a 1940s star? Do you exude the confidence of a contemporary force?

Your hair today represents the Femme Fatale spirit that lasts forever. What story does your hairstyle tell?

Make Up as an Art Form; The Femme Fatales Creative Palette

Now let's delve into one of the aspects; makeup! Smoky eyes, dark lips, and sculpted cheeks transform your face into a canvas waiting to be adorned. However, it's crucial not to overdo it and risk appearing like a caricature. Your makeup should enhance rather than conceal your feminine energy.

Are you prepared to create your masterpiece? Your canvas awaits its transformation.

Practicality Meets Allure; The Femme Fatale Wardrobe

Mastering the Femme Fatale look requires a curated collection of garments that strike a balance between practicality and allure. Think pieces that seamlessly transition from day to night from office hours to date nights.

Some essential items to consider are a fitted blazer, tailored trousers, and an elegant, sophisticated evening dress. Your wardrobe serves as your toolbox and a savvy Femme Fatale knows how to choose the tool, for each occasion.

Knowing when to splurge and when to save is key in Femme Fatale economics. Let's face it not everyone can afford a closet of designer labels. But here's the secret; you don't. Mastering the Femme Fatale look is about knowing when it's worth investing in pieces and when you can find budget-friendly alternatives that still match your style. It's not about the brand; it's, about how you carry yourself.

Here's the thing; being a Femme Fatale isn't limited to one body type or age group. It transcends norms. Applies to women of all shapes, sizes, and ages. Don't let anyone dictate what you should or shouldn't wear based on standards. Customize your Femme Fatale style according to your body shape and embrace it with confidence.

Remember this; the allure of a Femme Fatale knows no bounds of age or size – it remains timeless.

She represents the version of yourself that you could become if you have the dare her.

Final Thoughts; Embarking on Your Journey, as a Femme Fatale Now that you have all the strategies at your disposal it's time to put them into action. Start experimenting, selecting, and cultivating your Femme Fatale appearance. As you practice more it will begin to feel more natural bringing you closer to perfecting your style of mysterious feminine allure. Are you ready to leap? I think so. Your journey, as a Femme Fatale is about to commence. The world won't know what hit it.

FEMME FATALE BEHAVIOR AND MANNERISMS

The Golden Rule; Embrace Subtlety

Listen, being a Femme Fatale is not, about being loud or overly forceful. No, it's all about those gestures that speak volumes. A lingering gaze, a smile, a turn of the head. These are her hidden codes.

Pro Tip; Master the art of "less is more." Subtlety will take you further than any action.

Confidence is Your Greatest Asset; Walk with Conviction

You've probably heard this times. Confidence is crucial. However, for a Femme Fatale, it's like a currency. The way you walk, sit or even stand should radiate confidence. Imagine a thread pulling you up from the top of your head. Keep your posture straight with your shoulders. Pulled back slightly and let your hips sway naturally as you move.

Your Move; Practice your stride and your posture. How you sit. Remember, a Femme Fatale never slumps or slouches.

Eye Contact; Your Secret Weapon

Meaningful eye contact can be more intimate, than the kiss.

Lock eyes with someone for a moment, then usual and you've already set the stage for a powerful connection. But be careful;

there's a balance between being alluring and coming across as creepy.

Here's the scoop; Take some time to practice maintaining eye contact in front of a mirror. Get comfortable with the intensity so that it becomes natural for you.

Voice Modulation; The Enchanting Spell

Let's chat about your voice – it can. Be like a spell or lead to a shipwreck. A Femme Fatale speaks in a way that captivates others. Her voice is usually lower, softer, with a rhythm. She knows the power of pausing, the allure of sharing whispered secrets.

The Golden Rule; Less is more. Say what needs to be said. Let those pauses speak on your behalf.

Listen and Respond; The Art of Conversation

Conversations with a Femme Fatale are never one-sided. She excels at listening which is one of her skills. She makes the other person feel like they are the focus in the room giving them her attention.

Insider Tip; Practice listening. Show interest, in others. Respond in ways that keep the conversation flowing smoothly.

Non-Verbal Communication; The Unspoken Dialogue

It's fascinating how much you can convey without saying a word. Your body language plays a role, in communication. When you listen tilt your head slightly use your hands subtly to emphasize points or lean in to create a sense of intimacy.

Your Mission; Be aware of the conversation happening through your body language. It can speak volumes louder than words.

Master the Art of Flirting; Light Unexpected

Flirting is an art that thrives on being playful, enjoyable, and full of surprises... Remember there's a distinction between being flirty and desperate. A Femme Fatale never crosses that line.

Key Strategy; Master the art of implying rather than stating directly and hinting without confirming everything. Keep others guessing about your intentions.

Boundaries; Recognize Them Establish Them Embrace Them

A Femme Fatale never allows herself to be taken advantage of easily. She knows her worth. Firmly establishes her boundaries while maintaining gracefulness. It's all about striking a balance between allure and self-respect.

The Rule; Your boundaries are sacred; make them known to others. Never compromise them for anyone under any circumstances.

Don't Reveal Everything; Preserve the Element of Mystery

Maintaining an air of mystery is crucial to your persona. You don't have to be a book, for everyone; instead, choose what you share with whom.

A bit of intrigue can go a long way, in keeping people interested.

Honest conversation; Keep them curious. Give them hints, not the story.

Emotional Intelligence; Your Secret Superpower

Understanding cues, emotions and even the atmosphere in a room is your superpower. Utilize this intelligence to navigate social dynamics skillfully.

The Strategy; Always gauge the situation. Adjust your behavior to match the atmosphere and the people around you.

Authenticity; Stay True to Yourself

It may sound contradictory but within this crafted persona it's crucial to have a foundation of authenticity. People can easily spot a phony from away. So, embrace the Femme Fatale persona while staying true to who you're

Final Thought; Authenticity is captivating. Be an individual rather than just playing a role.

Take Control; Act Not Reactively

Let's be clear about something; A Femme Fatale doesn't wait for life to happen; she makes life happen. She takes the initiative of reacting. If she desires something or someone, she takes the steps to attain it.

Listen Carefully; Don't react when life throws situations at you; be proactive and take charge by creating opportunities yourself.

Mind Games; A Two-Sided Coin

It's important to approach mind games with caution. While they can add an element it's essential to use this tool ethically. The aim here is not manipulation; it's, about creating fascination.

The Ethical Guide; Utilizing mind games to maintain your air of mystery rather than manipulating others.

Closing Remarks; Embrace Your Inner Femme Fatale

So, you've perfected the look. Mastered the art of seduction. What comes next? Embodying it fully living and breathing as a Femme Fatale. Remember, this is not a role you slip into occasionally; being a Femme Fatale is an extension of who you truly are... Let's be honest why would you want to be anyone? You're magnetic, irresistible, and unforgettable as a Femme Fatale.

Always remember that embracing the behaviors and mannerisms of a Femme Fatale doesn't mean becoming someone it means revealing the captivating woman that has always been within you.

CRAFTING YOUR FEMME FATALE NARRATIVE

Your Story Matters. An Age-Old Tale

Let's get one thing straight; You're not meant to be a supporting character, in someone's Story. No, my dear, you are the protagonist, the inspiration, and the storyteller of your journey.

So, let's get ready to roll up our sleeves and explore the narrative elements that define who you truly are. What archetype do you embody? Discovering your Femme Fatale DNA involves identifying the traits and tendencies that shape your actions. Throughout history, Femme Fatales have taken on roles, like adventurers, nurturers, rebels, and sages. This section will help you understand your core characteristics and demonstrate how to utilize them to your advantage.

Have you ever wondered why captivating Femme Fatales exude an aura of mystery and intrigue? It's because they possess a backstory that adds depth to their allure. You don't have to invent a past for yourself. It is important to appreciate the richness of your own experiences and incorporate them into your narrative.

In this era branding isn't solely reserved for products; it extends to individuals as well. Learn how to shape a brand that reflects your Femme Fatale persona using the timeless pillars of persuasion; Logos (Logic) Ethos (Ethics) and Pathos (Emotion Let 's sets captivate your audience—whether it's an individual or a whole crowd—and make them fully invested in you.

Chapter; Mastering the Art of Conversation and Storytelling

If life were a stage our words would be our lines. We've already covered how to speak with allure. What about the content? This chapter equips you with a range of techniques that not only enhance your charm but also deepen your storytelling abilities.

Your Circle of Influence; Nurturing Relationships that Shape Your Narrative

No one can exist in isolation. The people we surround ourselves with be it lovers, friends, or rivals play roles in shaping our stories. Learn how to identify those who enrich your narrative and how to navigate those who might hinder it. You'll discover strategies for rewriting relationships. Gracefully cutting ties when necessary.

Plot Twists; Dealing with Life Challenges

Life often throws us curveballs, but a true conversationalist knows how to handle them and use them to their advantage. This section provides you with strategies for staying true, to your narrative when faced with unexpected twists and turns.

The Climax; Defining Moments that Shape Your Persona

Every story has its moment. The moment that tests the protagonist's mettle. What will yours be? It's impossible to predict. You can prepare yourself by developing the skills and mindset needed for such defining moments.

Uncover the secrets to gracefully navigating high-stakes situations ensuring that no matter what unfolds you emerge victorious.

The Epilogue; A Story That Never Ends

Spoiler alert; There is no conclusion, to your captivating Femme Fatale tale. Why? Because you're in a state of evolution adding chapters as you journey along. This isn't about putting on a show; it's about embracing a multifaceted identity that truly belongs to you.

BUILDING YOUR FEMME FATALE SKILL SET

Hello there individual! By now you have mastered the art of Femme Fatale fashion, behavior, and mannerisms. However, let me share a secret with you. Even if you have all those elements down pat there is still one piece missing from the puzzle; your narrative. Being a Femme Fatale isn't about appearances or actions; it's, about creating and embodying a story—a legend or myth—that keeps people irresistibly captivated and eagerly flipping through each chapter. Let's dive into the art of creating a Femme Fatale narrative.

The Background Story; Myth or Reality?

Something is captivating about a woman who exudes mystery and a touch of elegance. Whether you draw inspiration, from real-life experiences, or weave a past remember this; Your backstory doesn't define you. It adds layers to your enigmatic allure.

Keeping It Real; This isn't, about deception; it's selecting which aspects of your life you want to emphasize or elaborate on.

The Quirks; Standing Out in Style

Unique quirks or habits can make you truly memorable. Do you always have a go-to cocktail? Have a signature perfume? Use these elements to shape your persona.

Pearl of Wisdom; People tend to remember details so make sure you incorporate some quirks that are simply unforgettable.

The Catchphrase; A Life Tagline

Think of something that encapsulates your personality in a thought-memorable way—something you often say or could say.

Quick Tip; Your catchphrase should be catchy (obviously). Also deeply aligned with the essence of being a Femme Fatale.

The Trusted Confidant; A Reliable Companion

Femme Fatales require a confidant, someone who truly understands the person beneath the facade. Choose wisely; this individual can enhance your allure by safeguarding your secrets.

Caution; opt, for someone who comprehends the power of silence much as you do.

Goals and Ambitions; Drive is Alluring

Your story must encompass goals or aspirations whether it's achieving dominance or being the best in your field. Ambition is not only attractive but also captivating.

Manifesto; Know what you desire and fearlessly pursue it while allowing your ambitions to be a part of your narrative.

Emotional Depth; Layers upon Layers

Femme Fatales are never one dimensional. They possess layers that expose their vulnerabilities making them relatable and human.

Heart to Heart; Reveal glimpses of your complexity in moderation; it enhances your mystique without compromising your strength.

The Arch Nemesis; Drama Brings Depth

Think about any character and oftentimes they have a nemesis or at least a formidable opponent. This isn't about creating adversaries; it's, about facing challenges that make you stronger.

Life Lesson; Your story becomes more captivating when there is a challenge to overcome whether it is a person, an issue, or a personal obstacle.

Unexpected Twists; Keep Them Guessing

Life is ever-changing and so should your narrative. Keep your audience engaged by incorporating turns and surprises.

Surprise Element; Just when they think they have you all figured out change the game. That's the way of the femme fatale.

The Final Chapter; You Determine Its Conclusion

Your story doesn't come to an end just because others desire it. You hold the pen as the author; you decide when it concludes.

Closing Act; When you choose to transition or reinvent yourself make sure it is, on your terms.

Your Legacy; Leave Them Yearning for More

Femme fatales are unforgettable. Even after the last page is turned your tale continues to linger in the minds of those captivated by you.

Curtain Call; Always leave them yearning for more because a femme fatale never truly disappears; she patiently awaits her entrance.

Coming Up Next; Unveiling Dark Feminine Secrets

Having mastered the skills of being a femme fatale prepare yourself for exploring the secrets that fuel this allure.

Get ready, for some mind-blowing revelations, in the chapters. Hold on tight because this is going to be a journey you won't want to miss out on!

CHAPTER 3

DARK FEMININE SECRETS

THE PSYCHOLOGY BEHIND THE SECRETS

*H*ello there captivating enigma! Secrets seem to be your specialty, don't they? Whether it's a talent or a passion you keep hidden away secrets have this ability to transform you from an ordinary individual into a legendary Femme Fatale... Have you ever wondered what makes secrets so alluring? Get ready my diva because we're about to delve into the psychology, behind secrets.

The Temptation of the Forbidden

The concept of something being forbidden has always held an allure. It's in our nature to be curious and drawn towards the unknown. By having secrets, you exude that sense of allure akin to a gem locked away in a treasure chest just waiting to be discovered.

Psychological Insight; The "Forbidden Fruit Effect" is not merely folklore; it's a phenomenon. We naturally desire what we can't or shouldn't have.

The Power of Scarcity; Less is

The less you reveal the people's curiosity intensifies. Similar, to limited edition items the scarcity of your secrets only heightens their appeal. When something becomes scarce its desirability skyrockets.

Observation; Have you ever noticed how diamonds are more sought after compared to stones?

Scarcity enhances the value. Your secrets hold worth like precious diamonds.

Intrigue Fuels Engagement

By withholding information, you create an air of anticipation and curiosity. It's akin, to reading a captivating novel; people will keep flipping the pages if they sense a revelation is around the corner.

Readers Note; Consider your life as an enthralling story. What elements would make someone eager to skip? That's the allure of secrets.

The Halo Effect; How Secrets Captivate Us

When you maintain an aura of mystery people fill in the gaps with their imagination... Guess what? They often attribute more positive qualities to you than you may possess. It's known as the Halo Effect. It works in your favor.

Lightbulb Moment; By being slightly elusive others can envision you in their colors — something everyone desires,

Emotional Investment; Hooked, Line, and Sinker

The more effort someone puts into unraveling your mysteries, the deeper their emotional attachment becomes... My friend's emotional investment equals power.

Tugging at Heartstrings; Once they've strived for it revealing a guarded secret binds them to you far stronger, than surface-level facts ever could.

The Duality; Secrets Don't Diminish Your Authenticity

You might have concerns that keeping secrets means you're not being yourself. However, secrets add depth to your personality. They make you intricate not artificial.

Authenticity Alert; Being multi-faceted doesn't make you dishonest; it makes you captivate.

The Endgame; Complete Control Over Your Story

By understanding the psychology, behind secrets you're not just adding allure; you're taking charge of your narrative. You determine the pace, the tone, and the revelations. You are the writer, director, and protagonist of your saga.

Directors Cut; Think of your life as a movie. Would you want to reveal the ending from the beginning?

GUARDING YOUR MYSTIQUE

Hello there enchanting queen of mystery! You've captured their attention with your allure. Crafted story. But let's face it; maintaining that sense of mystery isn't a one-time effort. It's an endeavor—a part of your captivating persona, as a femme fatale. So how can you ensure that irresistible enigma remains intact? Get ready because you're about to become the guardian of your mystique.

Your Boundaries; A Protective Barrier, not a Prison

Contrary, to belief boundaries aren't meant to restrict you; they liberate you by preserving your sense of mystery. Establish guidelines for what you share and with whom because not everyone deserves backstage access to your life.

Golden Rule; Boundaries are like fences that nurture the flourishing of your captivating garden rather than letting it wither away.

Keep Them Guessing; The Power of Uncertainty

An intriguing individual never reveals everything. Maintain an element of ambiguity. The allure lies not in what you disclose but in what you choose to keep hidden.

Magicians Secret; It's not just about the reveal; it's the art of creating an illusion that something significant is on its way.

The Social Media Mirage; Crafting a Carefully Curated Persona

Navigating media can be tricky. Share much. You risk diluting your mystique. Share little. You might fade into obscurity. The key? Cultivate a presence that sparks curiosity without being so enigmatic as to isolate others.

Digital Wisdom; Treat media as your Femme Fatale portfolio, rather than a personal diary.

The Power of Silence; Underestimated and Profound

Silence isn't devoid of substance; it holds answers within.

Sometimes staying silent can have an impact. Strategically using silence can leave others curious, contemplating, and craving, for more.

Value of Silence; Silence holds value. In your case, it's as precious as a diamond.

Selective Disclosure; The Art of Sharing Enough

Reveal a few secrets to chosen individuals and make them feel special... Here's the trick; share something that doesn't truly expose yourself. This way you maintain an air of mystery while creating a sense of closeness.

Illusion & Intrigue; Offer them a glimpse behind the scenes but never reveal the stage.

Time Management; Your Presence is a Privilege

Don't always be readily available. It's supply and demand economics. The less you offer the more desirable you become.

Eternal Truth; Your time is an investment; spend it wisely. Let others know that sharing it with you is a privilege.

Emotional Poker Face; Guard Your Feelings

Being completely open about every emotion doesn't make you authentic; it makes you predictable. Keep your emotions protected not as a defense mechanism but, as a strategy to enhance your allure.

Feeling Fantastic; It's completely normal to experience emotions. It's wise to have control, over when and how you express them.

The Unexpected Vanishing Act; Leave Them Longing for

Now and again take a break without any explanation. When you return, you'll notice that your absence has sparked fondness or at the least heightened curiosity.

The Magic of Disappearing; Sometimes the best trick you can pull off is to vanish and then reappear as if by magic reigniting intrigue.

THE ART OF BEING UNPREDICTABLE

The Allure of Surprise; Why Unpredictability Holds Such Appeal

Let's dive in and explore why being unpredictable is such a deal. You know those cliffhangers at the end of your TV series? The ones that make you click on "Next Episode" even if it's way past your bedtime? That's the power of unpredictability. Now it's in your hands.

The Strategy of Predictability; Knowing When to Embrace Unpredictability

Unpredictability isn't about being chaotic or unstable; it's like a dance. Find those moments, in interactions, relationships, and even your career where sprinkling a little unpredictability will yield the greatest rewards.

Breaking Patterns; Adding a Dash of Surprise

Repeating patterns leads to predictability. Want to grab attention?

Discover the art of disrupting patterns in conversations, appearances, and behaviors. Gain insights, on how to surprise others by defying their expectations.

Become a master of misdirection like magicians, spies, and femme fatales. Learn techniques to divert attention from your intentions captivating people and keeping them off balance. By mastering this skill, you won't only be guarding secrets; you'll be shaping the narrative.

Unleash the power of ambiguity by speaking in riddles that leave room for interpretation. Explore how to communicate with the amount of uncertainty that sparks curiosity and captivates imaginations. You won't simply converse; you'll enchant others with your words.

Why limit yourself to one area of expertise when you can become a Swiss Army knife? Embrace interests, hobbies, and skills not only to enrich your own life but also to keep others intrigued. The broader your range becomes, the layers you add to your persona.

Learn how to keep people hooked using the reward system—like gambling machines and social media apps do. Discover how this principle can be applied in your interactions, for engagement.

Prepare to get hooked like you would with the captivating smartphone game! It's a compliment if someone has ever told you that you're difficult to understand. This section will guide you in expressing a range of emotions leaving others both baffled and captivated. You'll become an actress of an Oscar, in the movie that is your own life!

Next up; Discover how keeping secrets can enhance your aura.

You've truly mastered the art of being unpredictable. Now everyone wants to experience the thrill ride that's you. No one can quite figure you out. Ready to delve? In this chapter, we'll explore not only how keeping secrets maintains your air of mystery but also intensifies your hidden feminine power.

WHY KEEPING SECRETS ENHANCES YOUR DARK ENERGY

The Allure of the Unknown; Your Hidden World

Let's start by laying some groundwork; and understanding why the unknown holds such an appeal. Throughout history from exploring oceans to unraveling legends humans have always been fascinated by what lies beyond our knowledge... Guess what? You possess your realm of hidden depths waiting for exploration and safeguarding.

The Exclusivity Factor; The VIP Lounge within Your Soul

Imagine your secrets as a VIP lounge, within the nightclub that represents your life.

Not everyone has the privilege of access. This section discusses the impact of maintaining a sense of exclusivity, which enhances your allure and creates a space due, to its availability.

The Silent Influence; The Power of Hidden Knowledge

Having secrets grants you power. The power that comes from possessing information cultivating mystery and leveraging emotions. Explore the frameworks that explain why individuals with secrets often hold an undeniable influence over others.

Complex Emotions; Unveiling Layers of Identity

Secrets are not merely facts kept hidden; they encompass emotions, memories, and intricate layers that shape our persona. We will delve into how harboring secrets adds depth to one's character making them more complex and consequently captivating.

Forbidden Desires; The Seductive Side of Secrecy

Let's discuss how secrets can be undeniably alluring. From glance to veiled conversations the art of concealing something transforms interactions into something charged with electricity. Learn to wield this captivating tool with finesse.

The Esoteric Connection; Ancient Wisdom and the Art of Concealment

Have you ever wondered why many ancient societies had schools and teachings? We will explore how secrecy has been associated with wisdom and power throughout history allowing you to tap into this age practice.

The Mirror and the Mask; Personal Secrets, versus Public Secrets

Not all secrets are meant to be shared. It's important to understand the balance between keeping secrets for yourself and keeping them hidden from others. While one adds depth to your image the other strengthens your relationship with yourself.

Polarity in Relationships; The Power of Mystery

like a magnet requires both a north and south pole relationship need polarity to maintain attraction. We will explore how keeping aspects of yourself undisclosed can sustain or reignite the spark in types of relationships. Whether they're romantic, platonic, or professional.

Up Next; Techniques, for Building Lasting Confidence

You have mastered the art of unpredictability. Recognize the significant role that secrets play in enhancing your mysterious energy. Are you ready to showcase this newfound complexity and allure? Stay tuned because that's what we'll be delving into next!

CHAPTER 4

BOOSTING YOUR CONFIDENCE

INNER CONFIDENCE VS. OUTER SHOW

*T*he Deceptive Nature of Confidence; Unmasking the Illusion

Have you ever encountered someone who appeared self-assured only to discover it was all an act? Let's delve into the reasons behind this façade and how to recognize the signs of false confidence. Don't settle for superficiality; aim for authenticity.

The Root of Inner Confidence; A Journey Within

Confidence goes beyond surface-level appearances; it emanates from your core, your essence. Let's deeply explore where confidence originates and how to nurture this spark within your soul.

The Art of Presentation; Projecting Confidence in Crucial Moments

Sometimes it's necessary to "fake it till you make it." Learn techniques, for displaying confidence when it truly matters, whether you're giving a significant presentation going on an important date or simply enjoying a night out with friends.

A Symbiotic Connection; How One Boosts the

Guess what? Inner confidence and outward display aren't mutually exclusive. They complement each other in a cycle that fosters growth and undeniable allure.

Discover the secrets to establishing a connection, between yourself and your outward appearance ultimately boosting your self-assurance.

When it comes to our feelings and external presentation there is often a gap. However, you can bridge this gap by implementing strategies that align both aspects of yourself.

Your physical presence speaks volumes about your confidence level. From body language to clothing choices and mannerisms, they all contribute to telling a story. Explore techniques on how to ensure that your physical self reflects the confidence within you forming a narrative.

Having confidence is one thing. Putting it into action is another step. Learn insights on how to utilize your newfound confidence in conquering challenges of any size.

Contrary, to belief vulnerability, can be an indicator of inner confidence. This section will guide you through embracing openness in your personality without compromising the depth of your energy.

SELF-ACCEPTANCE: LOVING THE DARK AND LIGHT

The Reflection of Duality; Embracing Facets

Who said we must limit ourselves to one aspect? Let us embrace the idea that we can be both enchanting and nurturing, seductive and wise. Discover how these contrasting traits can coexist harmoniously within you.

Exploring the potential, within us explores those hidden aspects of ourselves that may not be fully embraced by society. By embracing these parts, we not become more captivating. Also, tap into a potent reservoir of energy that amplifies our femme fatale persona.

Sunlight and Shadows; The Dance of Oppo, sites

Ah, the dance, between opposing forces. Explore how your light attributes can complement and highlight your elements and vice versa. It's like having a yin-yang relationship within yourself that captivates the world.

The Gift of Self-Compassion; Your Supportive Critic

Being a femme fatale doesn't make us immune to self-doubt or criticism. Learn the art of self-compassion treating yourself with the kindness and understanding you would offer a friend.

Embrace Your Journey; Embracing Your Unique Story

Every scar every mistake and every triumph has shaped you into the individual you are today. Discover the significance of embracing your narrative, including both the chapters that fill you with pride and the ones that you may wish to modify.

Hidden Aspects; Embracing Every Part of Yourself

We all have aspects of ourselves that we prefer to ignore or keep hidden, don't we? But here's something to consider – even those parts deserve love and acceptance. This section serves as a guide, to embracing and accepting all aspects of yourself the ones you may have concealed away.

Transformation; The Magic of Self-Acceptances

Let's delve into something a bit shall we? Explore the power of self-acceptance, where your doubts can be transformed into self-assurance through the alchemy of unconditional self-love.

Holistic Self Care; Nurturing Both Sides

Self-care goes beyond indulging in bubble baths and spa days. It also involves doing shadow work and engaging in introspection. Learn tips on how to nourish both your darker and lighter sides lovingly.

What's Next; Strategies, for Cultivating Enduring Confidence

You've embarked on a journey of self-discovery now what comes next? In our chapter, we will explore strategies for solidifying this self-acceptance by cultivating lasting confidence.

STRATEGIES FOR BUILDING LASTING CONFIDENCE

The Secret, to Lasting Confidence; What Keeps It Going?

Let's start by unraveling the science behind lasting confidence. Is it something we inherit? Is it about adopting the habits? Brace yourself for an eye-opening experience that will challenge what you thought you knew about self-assurance.

Personal Affirmations; Your Cheerleaders

Words hold power. When we repeat the right ones, they can have a remarkable impact on our confidence levels. Discover how to create personalized affirmations that will keep you motivated and ready to tackle any challenge.

Small Goals, Big Rewards

Ever heard of the effect? In this section, you'll learn how achieving small manageable goals can trigger a series of successes that ultimately lead to a boost, in confidence. Get ready to achieve victory time and time!

Expanding Your Comfort Zone; Embracing the Exciting Unknown

Boredom is the archenemy of confidence. That's why we're going to shake things up. Learn how to intentionally step outside your comfort zone and embrace challenges that both excite and terrify you. Spoiler alert; You're more capable than you realize.

Strike a pose it's as simple, as that with an added confidence boost, of course! Explore scientifically supported power poses that not only improve your posture but also enhance your self-assurance. Who wouldn't want to feel like they're in Vogue?

Are you harnessing the potential of fashion? Fashion is a tool. Understanding its psychology can help you dress for success and increase your confidence and achievements.

Confidence has an effect. It's exhilarating to see how it can inspire those around you. Master the art of being a role model for self-assurance. Enjoy the confidence boost that comes with it.

In a world driven by gratification let's explore the importance of cultivating confidence. Like adopting eco habits learn how to maintain your self-assurance in the long run.

OVERCOMING INSECURITIES WITH DARK ENERGY

Before we bid them farewell let us acquaint ourselves with these party crashers known as insecurities. Delve into the root causes of your insecurities to understand why they've chosen to take residence within you.

Oh. Then we'll have to let them know that they need to leave their place of residence.

The Balance Between Light and Dark; How Dark Energy Complements Light

Darkness isn't the absence of light that sits with it. Discover how your insecurities can serve as a backdrop, for showcasing an intricate version of yourself. Your dark energy will bring out the depths of your character making you incredibly captivating.

Embracing Your Imperfections; Embracing the Real You

Whoever claimed that shadows are less significant than the objects casting them? Explore how embracing your flaws can act as a counterbalance to your insecurities.

Remember, your darker side is what sets you apart, and that holds power.

Seeing Insecurities in a New Light; Shifting Perspectives

Words and perspectives hold influence. Learn about the Mirror Trick, a technique that reframes the narrative around your insecurities by harnessing energy as a catalyst for transformation. Believe me when I say it's like witnessing magic unfold before your eyes.

Transforming Fear into Motivation; The Alchemy of Emotions

What if I told you that you could convert your insecurities, fears, and all those hidden aspects into fuel, for growth? This isn't thinking; it's emotional alchemy. Discover how to utilize your energy in reviving this practice for modern times.

Dark Charisma; Embracing Vulnerability as a Strength

Let's face it; allowing yourself to be vulnerable can be captivating. Having a side doesn't mean you're invincible; it means you're undeniably human. Discover how to harness vulnerability to your advantage without compromising your charm.

The Power of Authenticity; Being Genuine, in an Artificial World

Pretending to be confident can only take you far. Delve into why genuine dark energy serves as your shield against insecurities. Sets you apart in a world full of pretense.

Coming Up Next; Exploring the Stages of Seduction

Well, aren't you just soaking up wisdom? With your insecurities transformed into strengths, you're ready to venture into the thrilling realm of seduction. Keep those eyes open my dear because things are about to become more exhilarating.

CHAPTER 5

SEDUCTION AND RELATIONSHIPS

HOW TO SEDUCE ANY MAN

*C*reating an Irresistible Prelude; Setting the Scene

They say first impressions are crucial and oh boy we're going to make it unforgettable. Learn how to set the stage for the performance that's you. Fragrance, music, ambiance – it will be an experience, like no other! The Allure of the Femme Fatale Gaze; Eyes that Speak Volumes

Don't underestimate the power of your eyes to communicate. Discover the art of "the gaze," a captivating look that can convey much without saying a word... Remember it's, about mastering the technique and we've got you covered.

The Impact of Touch; Igniting a Spark

A touch can send shivers down someone's spine. Learn how to use touch not only as a connection but also as an emotional language. This is where your mysterious feminine energy truly comes into play.

Verbal Charm; The Art of Seductive Conversation

Seduction goes beyond attraction; it's about engaging someone's mind too. Explore the phrases, compliments, and conversational techniques that will make him think about you long after the conversation ends.

Secrets; Keeping Him Intrigued

We're diving into enigma mode here. A touch of mystery can make you utterly captivating so discover how to strike the balance between revealing and concealing. Make him work for those secrets. He'll be irresistibly drawn to you.

The Temptation of Unavailability; Playing Hard to Get

Why chase something that's always within reach? Learn why being, out of grasp can make you incredibly desirable.

This is not, about playing games; it's about positioning.

In this era, seduction has taken on a new form through texts, calls, and social media platforms.

Welcome to the world of Seduction 2.0. The electronic screens we hold can. Provide glimpses into ourselves or become captivating sources of attraction. Unravel the hidden meanings behind messages and online statuses that drive men wild.

The phenomenon of chemistry and its mysterious allure is, like energy. It possesses a power that can be harnessed in the bedroom or wherever your adventures may lead you.

THE FIVE PHASES OF SEDUCTION

Stage 1; The Introduction. Making a Memorable Entrance

Your grand arrival is more than stepping into a room; it's an announcement, a declaration that you've arrived. Learn how to create an impression that acts as a delightful appetizer to the wonderful person you are.

Stage 2; The Magnetic Attraction. Igniting the Spark

You know that moment when your eyes meet. It feels like the world around you has faded away. That's the magnetic attraction stage. It's more powerful than any aphrodisiac. Master the techniques to turn that curiosity into something.

Stage 3; The Deep Dive. Emotional and Intellectual Bonding

Now we're diving into waters, where minds connect and souls converse. Discover how to nurture an intellectual bond that makes him feel seen understood and completely captivated.

Stage 4; Physical Escalation. When Touch Speaks Volumes

This is where the magic happens— literally. Explore how to expertly escalate touch and closeness stirring up excitement and creating the setting, for irresistible sexual chemistry.

Stage 5; The Climax. Leaving a Lasting Impression

No, it's not what you might be thinking... Maybe it is! The climax phase goes beyond the aspect; it represents the culmination of all your efforts leaving a lasting impression. Discover how to make your exit as unforgettable, as your entrance leaving him eager for more.

The Ethical Femme Fatale. Embracing Responsible Seduction

Remember, having power also means having responsibility. Master the art of seduction because let's be honest toying with someone's emotions without care is no longer in vogue.

Transitioning from Seduction to Something That Comes After?

The initial dance of seduction can evolve into something if that's what you desire. Learn how to smoothly transition from being an enchantress to becoming a woman he cannot imagine his life without.

Coming Up; The Intricacies of Mind Games and the Influence of Suggestion

We have exciting things in store. Our next chapter will uncover the intricacies of mind games. Explore how the power of suggestion can add a layer of allure to your seductive skills.

MIND GAMES AND THE POWER OF SUGGESTION

Subliminal Messaging; When Your Wink Speaks Volumes Without Words

Think verbal communication is your tool? Think again. Your body language, tone, and even the timing of your messages can convey messages that resonate deeply with the mind.

Let's explore the world of messaging, where even a slight wink can have a powerful impact.

The Push Pull Technique; Riding Emotional Waves

Have you ever wondered why we are drawn to situations? It's because of the exhilarating ups and downs the tension and release. Learn how to become a master of emotions, with the push-pull technique a strategy that will captivate him with every word, touch, and gaze.

Anchoring; Connecting Emotions to Moments

You know that feeling when a particular scent instantly takes you back in time? That's the power of anchoring. Discover how to create anchors that link experiences or feelings to your presence. He won't be able to explain why he feels so good around you; he just will.

The Intermittent Reward; The Allure of Unpredictability

Are you like a prize he can't help but chase? Delve into the psychology, behind rewards – it's what makes unpredictability so addictive. Learn how to infuse excitement into his life to keep him coming back for more.

Open Loops; The Intrigue of Unfinished Stories

Keep him intrigued by sharing tales, comments, or experiences that are deliberately left unfinished leaving him wanting more...Discover how these unresolved storylines create a void that only you can fill, sparking his imagination and leaving him anticipating the installment.

The Art of Language; When Words Transform into Magic

Words are letters until they are arranged in a way that resonates deeply. Familiarize yourself with Neuro-Linguistic Programming (NLP) techniques that can transform conversations into captivating enchantments.

The Power of 'Yet'; Proposing a Future Together

Planting the seed of possibility for a shared future can be just as enticing, as reveling in the moment. Learn how the simple word 'yet' can unlock a world of potential in his mind and have him envisioning a future with you.

Ethical Psychological Strategies; Embracing Responsibility

Remember, you are treading on the ground here. With power comes great responsibility and ethical considerations are crucial when delving into tactics.

What's Next; Sexual Attraction and Enigmatic Feminine Energy

So now that you've mastered the art of maneuvers are you ready to infuse that spark into the realm of chemistry? Brace yourself because our upcoming chapter will delve into the electrifying connection, between attraction and your enigmatic feminine energy.

SEXUAL CHEMISTRY AND DARK FEMININE ENERGY

The "It" Factor; Unraveling the Chemistry That Matters

We've all experienced that captivating moment when we lock eyes with someone, and time appears to stand... What is the secret, behind that special 'It' factor? Is it something? Scientific? Predestined, perhaps? Maybe it's an art form that can be mastered.

Sensual Energy; The Power Within

You possess an energy but are you harnessing it effectively during your romantic encounters? Discover how to channel that untamed energy and emit captivating vibrations that no man can resist.

Body Language; The Silent Language of Desire

Words become insignificant when your body becomes a symphony with each movement serving as a note. Explore the art of using body language to express desire, mystery, and an irresistible allure that will leave him yearning for more.

Mindful Sensuality; Embracing the Power of Presence

Have you ever heard the saying that the brain is the crucial sexual organ? Well, there's truth in those words. Learn the art of sensuality to cultivate an almost spiritual connection in your intimate moments—a connection that will leave both of you enchanted.

The Art of Teasing; Savoring Anticipation

Who says everything needs to be rushed? The key to creating chemistry lies, in mastering the art of anticipation—the sweet elixir that heightens desire and makes every moment even more fulfilling.

Tease him tempt him and take your time to make the main event truly memorable and enjoyable.

The Power of Your Voice; Setting the Mood with Sound

Your voice holds power just like your physical appearance. Discover how to modulate your tone choose your words carefully use sighs and even silence to create an experience, for him.

Unveiling Universal Desires; Exploring Archetypes

From the ingenue to the commanding dominatrix delve into the sexual archetypes that resonate with dark feminine energy. Let these archetypes inspire you to explore facets of your sexual persona.

Vulnerability as an Aphrodisiac; The Unexpected Allure

revealing a touch of vulnerability can all appeal. Learn how to strike a balance between being a temptress and a vulnerable woman to create emotional depth that he won't be able to resist.

Ethical Seduction; When Consent Is Key

Consent isn't just a requirement; it's the foundation of any sexual encounter. Ensure that your ventures, into chemistry are built on respect and desire.

What's Next; Mastering the Art of Seduction

Girl you're there. You've set the stage; now it's time to bring it all together.

Our upcoming chapter will delve into the art of captivating others transforming you into a force of nature.

MASTERING THE ART OF SEDUCTION

Recapping the Alluring Aspects

Let's start by revisiting the enticing elements you have gathered along your journey, such, as embracing allure, employing tactics igniting sexual chemistry, and more. Consider these tools your arsenal as this chapter will teach you how to utilize them like a professional.

The Initial Move; Crafting an Unforgettable Prelude

You never get an opportunity to make an impression. Learn how to create opening moves that leave an impact. Whether it's through a glance a touch or chosen words seize this moment to set the stage for an unforgettable experience.

The Mid Game; Sustaining Attraction

While first impressions are crucial maintaining that initial allure is vital; otherwise, you risk fading like a fling. Discover strategies for sustaining intrigue and deepening connections while simultaneously building up tension.

The Grand Finale; Securing Success, with Elegance

This is where you cross the finish line with grace and finesse. Looking to create an experience whether it's a night or a lasting connection? Discover the secrets to leaving everyone wanting more.

In the realm of seduction, less is more. Learn how to harness the power of subtlety and nuance to your advantage. Remember, it's not, about what you do; it's also about what you choose not to do.

Being in tune with intelligence is key when it comes to seduction. Understand the importance of reading your target cues and adapting your approach accordingly. This is not about manipulation. Rather a sign of being a seductress.

Why let the allure fade away? Whether you're, in a long-term relationship or starting anew learn how to Kindle. Maintain that spark. True seductresses understand that the art of seduction is a journey.

With power comes great responsibility – especially when it comes to seduction. It's crucial to act responsibly as you master these techniques. Your abilities are potent; use them wisely.

CHAPTER 6

POWER DYNAMICS AND MANIPULATION

POWER IN RELATIONSHIPS: AN OVERVIEW

*T*he Importance of Power; Revealing its Nature

We've often heard the saying that power corrupts. That's not entirely accurate in this context. It's crucial to comprehend power dynamics in any kind of relationship whether or otherwise. Let's take a look at this often misunderstood concept and prepare ourselves for some insights!

The Foundation of Power; Essential Elements You Shouldn't Ignore

Imagine relationships as a house and power as its foundation. How strong is your foundation? Trust, emotional connection, financial freedom, and even sexual compatibility are like bricks that contribute to the solidity of your house. So, let's start building that foundation

The Balance of Influence; Who Holds the Reins?

In every relationship, there exists a balance of influence. Sometimes it is evenly distributed; at times it may be skewed. The key, to maintaining a fulfilling relationship lies in understanding when to assert control and when to let go.

Strategic Moves; Playing Your Cards Right

Just as you wouldn't reveal all your cards during a high-stakes poker game the same principle applies in relationships.

Knowing when to be vulnerable when to maintain an air of mystery and when to challenge someone's bluff—this chapter serves as a guide, for those who take risks in relationships.

Emotional Intelligence; The Unseen Currency

Ah, emotions—the force behind every relationship. Understanding the cards, you hold can help you navigate situations. You'll discover how to become the envy of others by mastering wealth.

Negotiating with Confidence; Expressing Your Desires

As a captivating individual, it's only natural that you have desires. Learning the art of negotiation within a relationship is, like adding a pinch of spice to a dish—it elevates the experience.

The Power of Vulnerability; Embracing Softness

Wait did you say power through vulnerability? Absolutely! Never underestimate the strength that lies within revealing your side. Sometimes yielding holds more power than exerting force.

Beware the Dark Side; Ethical Use of Power

Just because you're stepping into your power doesn't mean it should be wielded carelessly. Remember, great power comes with responsibility—a lesson even Spider-Man understood well.

Looking beyond relationships the insights, you gain into power dynamics can have an impact, on various aspects of your life. Prepare yourself to make progress in family-related and even professional spheres, like you've never experienced before.

Social Manipulation: Dark Feminine Strategies

Let's talk about something that often goes unaddressed; the perception of "manipulation", as something... What if we looked at it from an angle? At its core manipulation can simply be seen as handling or control of a situation or person. As long as your intentions are good, and you approach it ethically being adept at navigating complex social dynamics can be a way to let's break free from judgment and explore these strategies that some may consider "dark feminine."

Think like a Chess Grandmaster; Embracing Strategic Thinking

Life is like a game of chess not checkers. It's your move! Of being a pawn on the board think like the queen who plans several moves. In this case, you'll learn how to develop foresight. Imagine yourself at a party or in a business meeting – you'll discover how to see the picture understand connections between people identify individuals and position yourself strategically for success. It's all, about making those winning moves! The Subtle Power of Non-Verbal Cues

Sometimes it's not necessary to shout to make yourself heard; a gentle whisper can often have an impact. Discover the art of cues whether it's a look, a casual touch, on someone's arm, or even how you position your body during a conversation. By mastering these signals, you will become skilled in the language of verbal communication.

Emotional Intelligence; Your Secret Weapon

I cannot emphasize enough how crucial Emotional Intelligence (EI) is when it comes to navigating interactions. Being able to understand and adapt to contexts is invaluable. It's like having X-ray vision into people's emotions and motivations that are hidden beneath the surface. In this section, I will provide you with the tools to enhance your EI so that you can effectively navigate any setting.

Crafting Your Social Persona; The Art of Presenting Yourself

What you choose to reveal may not always reflect who you truly are. Developing a persona is not about being fake; rather it involves highlighting aspects of your genuine self based on the situation, at hand. Like a chameleon, you will learn how to blend in when needed and shine brightly when it's time to take the stage.

Mirroring and Projection; Unlocking Deep Connections

Want people to instantly warm up to you? Imitate their body language, the way they speak, and even their interests to an extent. Similarly, projection is a technique that involves showcasing the qualities you want others to perceive in you. In this section, we will delve into the science, behind these tools for establishing a connection.

The Carousel Technique; Keep Them Guessing

There is something truly captivating about unpredictability. While people may desire stability, they often crave the thrill of not knowing what lies ahead. Learn the Carousel Technique to maintain interactions that are predictable enough to build trust but also sporadic enough to preserve allure.

Escaping the Trap; Navigating Negative Manipulation

As you wield your newfound capabilities you may encounter situations where manipulation is directed towards you. How can you protect your energy? We will discuss exit strategies and defense mechanisms that will help safeguard your aura.

Practice, Practice, Practice; A Practical Guide for Daily Implementation

This isn't just talk; it's a skill set that requires practice. Similar, to practicing an instrument or engaging in a sport these strategies need to be exercised to do what? We are providing steps and exercises to ensure that you do that.

LEVERAGING YOUR DARK FEMININE ENERGY AT WORK

Leave behind the talk by the water cooler because it's time for a power-packed lunch break.

Ladies let's break through that glass ceiling. Let's do it with grace and sophistication. Who says the boardroom must be dull? Whether you're aiming for that corner office or already occupying it your unique feminine energy is your weapon to conquer your career ambitions. And I don't mean surviving; I'm talking about rising like the leader you are. Ready? Hold on tight things are about to get real.

Navigating Office Politics and Drama; Mastering the Game

Hate to burst your bubble. Workplace dynamics aren't all that different from high school cliques. Of math problems and cafeteria meals, we now have deadlines and team meetings. How can you skillfully navigate this maze? Your innate feminine energy can serve as your guiding compass helping you sail through challenging situations and leading you towards triumph.

The Power of Professional Attire; When Your Outfit Shouts CEO

We'll delve into understanding how colors affect our psychology explore the allure of fabrics and master the art of accessorizing. Let's face it. A powerful appearance can often convey more, than a crafted email.

Sure! Here's the paraphrased version;

Discover how to curate a wardrobe that exudes confidence and embraces a captivating charm.

Master the art of communication, in your quest for career success. Uncover strategies to employ language that showcases your strengths captivates attention and subtly influences outcomes. It's like being a wizard and guess what? You're the one with the magic.

Learn how to build connections in your network strategically. Identify individuals and power players within your workspace all while maintaining your authenticity and integrity.

Harness the power of your qualities without compromising yourself. Embrace your energy as an asset in navigating workplace dynamics. Think of it as an ace, up your sleeve that can dazzle, disarm, negotiate, and navigate with finesse.

Explore the concept of work-life balance — is it a myth or something achievable? Balancing a demanding career and a fulfilling personal life can feel like navigating a path especially when faced with challenges. So, what's the key, to finding harmony? Today we'll explore how tapping into your strength and embracing your energy can help you strike a balance between your professional and personal spheres... Guess what? It's what you might think!

Navigating Ethical Influence, in the Workplace

Yes, we're talking about "influence" again... This time let's dive into the ways to wield it within the context of work. Want to steer conversations during team meetings or gain an advantage in negotiations? There are honorable approaches that can help you achieve that.

Transitioning from Office Scapegoat to Stellar Professional

Last but certainly not least let's delve deep into transforming how others perceive you and improving your reputation at work. If you've ever felt unfairly pigeonholed or underestimated this roadmap will guide you towards redemption. Gaining the recognition you deserve.

Whew! That was quite an information-packed read, wasn't it? Fear not! Armed with these strategies you won't just be taking your place at the table; you'll be ready to lead those important meetings yourself.

When you enter your workplace or join a Zoom call time you won't just be a participant; you'll bring a presence. Embrace that energy, like a skilled professional. Your career will experience an impact. You'll be fully aware and in control. Until we meet again continue excelling at your tasks and exceeding expectations. Your future success is waiting for you.

CONFLICT RESOLUTION; THE DARK FEMININE WAY

Have you ever found yourself in an office environment where tension hangs heavily in the air? Take a moment to breathe. Remember, you are not the storm; instead, you embody the calm that follows it. It is equally important to know when to step as it's to know when to engage. Be attuned to the atmosphere of the room sense the energies present and let your intuitive feminine wisdom guide your actions. Consider it your superpower; utilize it!

Navigating Challenges, with Confidence; Realizing Your Inner Strength

Conflicts are inevitable; they are a part of life. Often arise within workplaces or relationships.

You have two options; Enter the battlefield without any weapons. Confidently embrace your high heels as tools of seduction. Which path will you choose?

The Art of Silence; Balancing Passive Aggressiveness and Strategic Reserve

There is a skill, in remaining silent. The strategic reserve is your power as a woman. It's not about being weak or passive; it's about selecting your battles and speaking up when your words will have an impact. Learn how to master the art of holding back and delivering statements at just the right moment like a well-aimed dagger.

Knowing When to Show Your Teeth; Assertiveness Without Becoming Overbearing

There is a time and place for everything for displaying your fierce determination... How can you do that without causing turmoil? It requires finding an equilibrium between assertiveness and grace, strength and composure. Let's discuss strategies that go beyond resolving conflicts; they can transform them into stones toward growth.

From Disorder to Charisma; Unleashing the Power of Feminine Alchemy

Conflict shouldn't be seen as a problem to solve; it holds the potential for transformation. This is where the enchantment of alchemy comes into play. By approaching conflicts, with wisdom, you can transmute them into charisma. Even turn adversaries into allies.

Your colleagues won't just admire you they'll be captivated. You're not simply resolving problems; you're captivating hearts.

The Power of Psychology and Emotional Intelligence; Your Secret Weapon

This goes beyond a game of cat and mouse; it's a dance and you take center stage. By utilizing your intelligence and intuitive understanding you can almost predict people's actions before they even make them. While they are playing checkers, you're playing a chess game.

Embrace Responsibility and Navigate Smoothly

Guess what? Sometimes conflicts may arise due to your actions. Yes, even queens stumble over their gowns occasionally... When this happens gracefully accepting responsibility can transform a conflict into an opportunity to build trust. Nothing showcases leadership more, than admitting mistakes and making amends.

Illuminate the Path of Burning Bridges

A conflict doesn't have to signify the end; it can be the start of something. Harness that intuitive energy to not resolve issues but forge stronger connections. Show others the way. Suddenly you're not just involved in the drama—you become the guiding force.

CHAPTER 7

SPIRITUAL CONNECTIONS AND PERSONAL GROWTH

THE DARK GODDESS. ARCHETYPES AND MYTH UNVEILING THE COSMIC BLUEPRINT

*W*elcome to a ballroom, where ancient Dark Goddesses become your enchanting dance partners. Brace yourself for an exhilarating experience! Have you ever wondered why certain stories, myths, or characters deeply resonate with your soul? Well, my friend, it's no coincidence; it's the power of energy and mythical resonance, at play. Within you lies the Dark Goddess eagerly waiting to reveal herself.

The Haunting and Inspiring Archetypes

Let's begin by delving into the realm of archetypes. Picture them as recurring roles or characteristics imprinted on humanity's consciousness throughout millennia. The Dark Goddess archetype embodies those aspects of femininity that often remain unspoken but hold power – intuition, mystery, transformation, and yes sexual energy. It represents a force within you as the moon itself and as instinctual, as the ebb and flow of tides.

The Living Legends

Prepare to meet some goddesses from mythology – fierce trailblazers who inspire awe in us all. From the Kali, in Hinduism to the Hecate in Greek mythology these are powerful women (or rather deities) who didn't hide in the shadows. They personified darkness. Embraced it. By exploring their stories you'll discover that the Dark Goddess is not just a villain ". A multifaceted figure embodying resilience, wisdom, and even a touch of the forbidden.

So why should you take an interest in these tales? Well, my dear friend, think of them as mirrors reflecting parts of yourself that you may not be aware of yet. Just like your reflection can reveal both your beauty and imperfections these myths can help you better comprehend your light and dark sides. It's like having your cosmic mirror tailored for and let me tell you it suits you perfectly.

Now I'm sure you're curious about how to tap into this Dark Goddess energy and infuse it into your life. Well lucky for you we're about to delve into some age practices with a twist. Think of it as spirituality, with a squeeze of lime. Tangy yet oh-so revitalizing.

"The Transformative Influence of Mythology

Understanding the presence of the Dark Goddess within yourself goes beyond contemplation; it becomes a profound and spiritual journey. Once you grasp the archetype that resonates with your being you will navigate life's challenges, with elegance, composure, and an undeniable inner strength that will capture the attention of others.

By the time you conclude, Dark Goddesses will have brought you one step closer to embodying their essence. You will possess a divinity, armed with wisdom and an irresistible mystical charm. So go ahead. Set free your goddess; let her dance freely under the enchanting moonlight that has long awaited her arrival.

And remember, the power of the Dark Goddess extends beyond circumstances; it resides within your everyday existence. It manifests itself in your gait, conversations, and in how you make people feel. Are you ready to tap into this energy? Without a doubt!"

SPIRITUAL PRACTICES FOR HARNESSING YOUR DARK ENERGY. YOUR COSMIC TOOLKIT FOR UNEARTHLY ALLURE

Are you prepared to infuse some age wisdom into your reality Let's not waste any time as your inner Dark Goddess eagerly awaits her entrance, with a cosmic VIP pass. By the end of this section, you'll have a toolkit that goes beyond spirituality and becomes downright magical. Get ready to infuse some stardust into your life.

Mindfulness with a touch of mystique

things let's talk about mindfulness. But hold on this isn't your mindfulness; it's mindfulness drenched in the captivating essence of the Dark Feminine. Imagine paying attention to every experience, every emotion, and every vibration that courses through you but doing it with the allure of a Femme Fatale. It's mindfulness that not only brings you into the moment but electrifies it.

Moon Rituals; Harmonizing with the Lunar Cycle

Have you ever noticed how the moon seems to captivate our imaginations and even influence our moods? Well, that's no coincidence. Your connection to energy is inherently intertwined with the lunar cycle. So let's synchronize your energy with the waxing and waning of the moon. From setting intentions during the New Moon to delving into your depths on Full Moon nights these rituals will serve as your monthly check, with your inner goddess.

Journaling; Unveiling the Secrets of Your Intrigue

It's time to dust off that journal of yours. This time let's infuse it with a touch of mystery. It's not, about jotting down your thoughts; it's about weaving the captivating story of your persona. Picture each entry as an incantation that enhances your intrigue, allure, and self-awareness.

Sacred Sexuality; Embracing the Sensual Artistry

Now comes the part—embracing your sexuality as a blessing. Whether you find yourself dancing alone in your sanctuary or sharing moments with a partner view each experience as a ceremony. This is where you truly embrace your power as a force cherishing every sensation and desire as an integral part of your divine essence.

Energy Work; Harnessing Your Inner Energies

Let's explore the realm of energy work encompassing chakra balancing, aura cleansing, and grounding practices. While some may consider these techniques unconventional even skeptics become believers once they feel the effects. Think of it as attuning your frequencies to resonate with the goddesses of ancient tales.

The Shadow Self; Embracing Your Darker Depths

Last but certainly not least let us delve into shadow work—a journey, towards befriending our darkness and exploring its depths.

You have hidden aspects of your mind that you may prefer not to explore. Guess what? That's where your raw strength lies. Shadow work involves the act of shedding light on your darkness transforming it into a source of resilience and wisdom.

Once you delve into this section you won't merely be practicing spirituality; you'll be living it breathing it and embodying it every day. Your connection, to the Dark Feminine Energy won't remain a concept; it will become a part of your lived experience. Brace yourself for a journey that's both captivating and enlightening... Always remember that you hold the power to transform the ordinary into something just like an alchemist does. So why wait? Your divine self is calling out to you.

THE EMPOWERING INFLUENCE OF SHADOW WORK; TRANSMUTING YOUR DARKNESS, INTO VALUABLE LESSONS

Hey beautiful soul! Let's dive together. We're going beyond surface-level charm. Venturing into the depths of your soul – exploring areas of your psyche that may have been overlooked. But don't worry; you won't be embarking on this journey consider me as your guide.

We're about to embark on a journey of transformation, where we'll take what you might perceive as your 'darkness and turn it into authentic power.

So, let's cut through the jargon for a moment; What is shadow work? Well, it's a concept coined by the psychiatrist Carl Jung. It refers to the process of recognizing, acknowledging, and integrating the less obvious or 'darker' aspects of your personality. Imagine your personality, as an iceberg; the shadow represents the submerged part that often goes unnoticed... Oh boy, that submerged treasure can be incredibly valuable!

Mirror, Mirror; Confronting Truths

Yes, indeed we're going to delve into those idiosyncrasies, fears, and tendencies that you'd rather keep hidden. This isn't about criticizing or judging yourself; it's about facing yourself in the mirror and accepting every aspect of who you are flaws and all. You see, by confronting these aspects can you harness their energy in a way. It's like befriending an animal that becomes your fierce protector once tamed.

Journal Prompts; Exploring Your Shadow Diary

No comprehensive toolkit for self-discovery would be complete, without some journal prompts specifically designed for shadow work.

Imagine this space as your confessional, a place where you can freely express your deepest secrets, fears, and hidden desires. Trust me when you externalize these thoughts their power, over you weakens and becomes material that you can work with.

Moving from Darkness to Light; The Process of Integration

Once you acknowledge your shadows the next step is to integrate them. This is where the fun begins – think of yourself as a chef blending aspects of your personality to create a modern and authentic version of yourself. Envision harmonizing your light and dark sides to create a blend of Femme Fatale vibes.

Daily Practices; Sustaining the Transformation

Shadow work is not a one-time event; it's a relationship with yourself. Let's discuss practices that will keep you connected with your shadow self. We're talking about meditations, affirmations, and mindfulness techniques specifically designed to maintain the balance between light and dark in your life.

Transformational Stories; The Rise of the Phoenix

To wrap things up let's share some captivating stories of women who have successfully navigated their shadows and emerged as versions of themselves. Think of these tales as boosts of inspiration that will keep you motivated during times, on your journey.

There you have it your guide to alchemy. By the end of this section, you'll become skilled, at transforming what some may perceive as 'imperfections and 'negative aspects into your strengths. Remember darkness is not the absence of light; it serves as the backdrop against which light shines brightly.

So go ahead. Delve within yourself to uncover the hidden treasures residing in your shadow self. Your Femme Fatale persona encompasses more than looks and cunning charm; it's about embracing and celebrating every aspect of your being whether it be light, dark, or somewhere in, between.

ASTROLOGY AND THE DARK FEMININE; HOW THE STARS SHAPE YOUR INNER FEMME FATALE

Hello enthusiast! Are you prepared to explore the realm of energy together and soar to celestial heights? Let's dive into astrology. You see the stars and planets can reveal insights about your dark feminine energy. It's not about checking your horoscope for love or money; it involves delving into the one-of-a-kind astrological imprint you were born with unveiling your inner Femme Fatale. Intrigued? Well, get ready for a journey through the cosmos!

The Birth Chart; Unveiling Your Celestial Blueprint

things first if you haven't already obtained your birth chart (also known as a natal chart) it's time to do so. Think of it as a blueprint—a snapshot of the sky now you entered this world. Numerous websites and apps can generate one for free. Simply input your birth date, time, and location, and voila! You'll be presented with a circle filled with symbols, lines, and numbers. Don't worry; we'll decipher its secrets together.

Femme Fatale Planets; Venus, Mars, and Pluto—Oh My!

Ah yes! These are the forces behind desire, allure, and power— the heavyweights, in our journey.

Venus represents beauty and attraction while Mars symbolizes passion and aggression... What, about Pluto? Well, that's the planet associated with transformation. You guessed it secrets! Understanding the positions of these planets in your chart can provide insights into how to harness your dark feminine energy. For instance, if you have Venus in Scorpio, it may suggest that you possess a charm. On the other hand, having Mars in Aries indicates that you are a go-getter who excels in both love and conflicts.

While your Sun sign holds significance have you ever explored your Moon sign? The Moon governs your realm. Can serve as a significant indicator of your dark feminine inclinations. If your Moon is in Capricorn, it might make you slightly guarded but exceptionally resilient.

On the other hand, a Moon in Pisces suggests that intuition and emotional depth are among your powerful dark feminine traits.

When discussing energy certain astrological houses play vital roles akin to stage settings for planetary performances. The 8th and 12th Houses are particularly relevant, in this context as they hold secrets and wield power.

These houses represent rebirth, transformation, secrets, and hidden aspects of the self. Hello Femme Fatale enthusiasts!

Astrological Aspects; Trines, Squares, and Conjunctions

Don't limit yourself to examining the positions of planets and houses; also consider the angles, between planets to understand how your energies interact dynamically. For example, a conjunction of Venus and Pluto can enhance your captivating allure making you irresistibly magnetic.

Tailor Your Femme Fatale Toolkit

Using your birth chart as a guide you can personalize your Femme Fatale toolkit according to your characteristics. You might incorporate crystals, mantras, or specific rituals that align with your energies to intensify your mysterious feminine aura.

Now you know it, all-star child. Your birth chart is not merely something to analyze; it holds insights that can assist you in harnessing your dark feminine energy. You are not an assortment of traits; instead, you are a celestial masterpiece radiating the essence of a Femme Fatale as written among the stars. So go ahead! Embrace this wisdom as a tool, for becoming the most enchanting version of yourself.

THE INTERSECTION OF FEMINISM AND DARK FEMININITY WHERE EMPOWERMENT MEETS ALLURE

Hello! You're quite the trailblazer! Before we delve into this topic let's clarify something away; Dark feminism and feminism go hand in hand. Yes, you can fully embrace that intriguing Femme Fatale persona while proudly proclaiming "girl power!", with all your might. Feeling a bit perplexed? Intrigued? Well, you should be! We're about to debunk some misconceptions and explore the captivating realm where feminism and dark femininity intertwine in an alluring dance.

Smashing the Patriarchy with a Dash of Seduction

Firstly, let's dispel the notion that embracing femininity somehow diminishes your values. Not! Feminism is about having the freedom to be whoever you want to be including a seductive force of nature. It's not anti-feminist to tap into your Femme Fatale; what's truly anti-feminist is believing that women should only fit into predefined societal molds. Want to captivate someone with a gaze? Go ahead! Want to lead a meeting or spearhead a movement? You have every capability for both. In fact, why not do both?

Embracing Empowerment through Mystery and Autonomy

The allure of femininity isn't, about surrendering power; it's about harnessing it in its enchanting form.

By keeping aspects of who you are hidden you retain control over how your story unfolds. Think about it for a moment. In a world that often tries to define women even before they have the chance to define themselves holding onto your secrets can be quite revolutionary.

Let's talk about the gaze," which often reduces women to mere objects, for male gratification. But here's something interesting; the Femme Fatale doesn't play by those rules. Her allure is purely for her pleasure. If men happen to find her captivating well that's a side effect of her fabulous existence. Do you see the difference? Your mysterious feminine energy isn't meant to please anyone but yourself. So, turn the tables. Let them all fall under the spell of your Femme Fatale gaze.

Now let me share with you feminism's secret; The Madonna Whore Complex. Society has always tried to pigeonhole women into categories like " girls" or "bad girls.". Who says you can't embody both or neither? The enigmatic feminine energy laughs in the face of this dichotomy. She is complex and multi-dimensional. Refuses to be confined by labels... Guess what? Feminism has been fighting this battle for a long – breaking free, from limiting beliefs and empowering women to embrace their true authentic selves.

Let's get real for a moment. Feminism is more, than about challenging the patriarchy; it's about fostering inclusivity for all women of their race, sexuality, or background. The realm of femininity follows the principle. Its mysteries, its attraction, and its strength are meant for everyone.

So, my empowered and captivating friend, whether you're there protesting with a "The Future's Female" sign or captivating others with your enigmatic presence remember this; Feminism and dark femininity can coexist and should come together. Together they create a force that challenges norms and empowers you to be authentically yourself. So go ahead. Merge these worlds – watch how you become a more mesmerizing version of yourself.

CHAPTER 8

LIVING AUTHENTICALLY

EMBRACING YOUR FULL SELF - THE RISKS AND REWARDS OF LIVING ON THE BOUNDARIES, BETWEEN LIGHTNESS AND DARKNESS

*H*ey there you radiant rebel! Are you ready to stop holding back who you truly are and fully embrace yourself? Well get ready because in this chapter we'll discuss both the advantages and challenges that come with living life to yourself – embracing both lightness and darkness energies.

Being completely authentic can often feel like playing a high-stakes game in a poker match. There's always that lingering possibility of losing friendships missing out on opportunities or not being accepted by society. However, there's also the chance of winning big; forming connections gaining unwavering self-confidence, and living a life that truly feels like your own. It's undeniably exhilarating, isn't it?

Let's dive into the aspects and the incredible rewards that come with embracing yourself and fully embracing your dark feminine energy.

1. True Connections; When you shed the masks and stop putting on a show something magical happens. You attract people who are genuinely drawn to you – not some curated version they see on social media.

2. Confidence; There's nothing, like the high you experience when you authentically be yourself and realize that you are more than enough just as you are.

3. Freedom; No longer wasting time and energy on maintaining a façade allows for an abundance of bandwidth. Just imagine all the things you could do!

On the side of this coin lie risks;

1. Social Backlash; It is important to acknowledge that not everyone will be enthusiastic, about your authenticity –. That's perfectly okay. Just be prepared for some raised eyebrows or even outright criticism.

2. Missed Opportunities; Sometimes when trying to be true, to yourself you might not fit into someone's Expectations whether it's a job, a relationship, or a social circle.

3. The Emotional Toll; Being authentic is. Can also take a toll. It requires courage to reveal your world.

Living Outside Your Comfort Zone

Living by embracing both your flaws and strengths can be like living on the edge of your comfort zone. Yes, it can be scary. The rewards are incredible. You'll discover aspects of yourself you never knew existed and unlock levels of fulfillment in life.

The Empowering "Who Cares?"

What if people talk? So, what if they have opinions on how you should live? Adopting a "Who Cares?" attitude allows you to confidently live life on your terms brushing off voices as easily, as removing lint from your favorite black dress.

Finding Balance; It's Not All About Drama and Mystery

A life lived to the fullest is exhilarating but also draining. Find equilibrium by embracing not only the aspects but also the nurturing and optimistic sides of yourself.

The Femme Fatale isn't just confined to the shadows; she also revels in the sunlight. Are you prepared to embark on a journey, into the captivating universe that defines who you are? I have a feeling you're. It may involve some risks. The potential rewards are boundless. Embrace yourself, flaws and all. Witness how the world unfolds before you in unimaginable ways.

CRAFTING YOUR BRAND OF DAINTY - DESIGNING YOUR FEMME FATALE PERSONA FROM SCRATCH

Hey there soul! Are you ready to delve into crafting a style for your inner Femme Fatale? No, we're not solely referring to your wardrobe (although that's definitely). We're about to explore how you can shape a brand that exudes an enchanting aura of dark femininity.

Why Crafting Your Brand is a Game Changer

Let's be real; in this era driven by media, we all represent ourselves as brands whether we realize it or not. Even if being an influencer or amassing followers isn't your goal, how you present yourself sends out a message. So why not be deliberate, about it? Make that message scream "Femme Fatale" in the most captivating way possible.

The Key Elements of an Irresistible Femme Fatale Brand

Before we dive into creating your captivating brand let's gather the elements. Here's what you'll need;

Intrigue; Every Femme Fatale thrives on a sense of mystery. You don't have to become a recluse. A touch of enigma goes away.

Charisma; Consider this your superpower. Your ability to captivate those, around you, leaves a lasting impression and keeps them coming for more.

Style; This encompasses your fashion choices, makeup, and even your digital aesthetic. It's how you visually communicate with the world.

Voice; This isn't about how you speak. Also, how you write, tweet, or engage on Instagram. Your voice sets the tone for how others perceive you.

Establishing the Foundation; Questions to Reflect On

What words would you want people to use when they describe you?

What makes you undeniably unique?

How committed are you to maintaining your Femme Fatale persona?

Who are your role models, in terms of being a Femme Fatale? What valuable lessons can be gleaned from them? Ladies this isn't, about playing dress up; it's about the power of psychology!

The colors you choose the way your clothes fit and how you accessorize all speak volumes even before you say a word. Whether you embrace a modern-day Morticia Addams vibe or prefer a laid-back boho sorceress look make sure your style aligns with the image you want to project.

Consistency is crucial; every little detail matters when it comes to amplifying your brand's impact. From the color scheme on your Instagram feed to how you sign off on emails maintaining consistency is like the glue that holds together your Femme Fatale persona.

Remember, being a Femme Fatale means knowing where to draw the line. Don't forget that overexposure can quickly kill off your air of mystery faster than a necklace does to a vampire. Keep them guessing. Always leave them wanting more.

Your brand isn't tone; it's like clay. It should. Grow with you as time goes on. New experiences, insights, and even shifts, in your feminine energy, should be reflected in how you present yourself.

Alright darling, have you tapped into your energy? Developing your style of captivating femininity goes beyond appearance; it's, about embracing the enchanting allure of a Femme Fatale that has always resided within you. Delve into thoughts approach it with a discerning mind and, above all savor the experience! The world is not prepared for the power you're about to unleash.

EMBRACING YOUR TRUEST SELF AND UNLEASHING YOUR POTENTIAL

Welcome to the culmination of our journey together. Trust me this is where things truly become transformative. You've already mastered the art of aesthetics cultivated an allure and delved into the secrets. However, all of this would be, in vain if you can't channel it toward becoming the woman you were meant to be. So, let's jump into it!

The Pursuit of Authenticity; Going Beyond the Persona

Let's be honest here being a Femme Fatale is like adopting a powerful persona. It's undeniably enticing. Still just a persona at its core. The real power lies in authenticity – merging your Femme Fatale qualities with yourself. While a persona can attract people initially it's yourself that keeps them hooked. That's where the magic happens.

The Inner Dialogue; Empowering Self-Talk

Hey lady! If you're anything like me there's this voice, inside your head that loves to offer commentary on everything. Sometimes it cheers you on like a cheerleader; at times it can be quite critical.

Let's tune in, to that wavelength. Ensure the messages you send yourself are ones that empower uplift and strengthen your Femme Fatale energy.

The Transformation Toolkit; Practices, Ceremonies, and Discoveries

Whether it's a meditation routine or a weekly pampering session incorporating rituals that nourish your soul can bring about shifts in your energy. It's not about what you do but about how it makes you feel. Rituals can ground you. Serve as reminders of your journey.

Overcoming Obstacles; Navigating Challenges and Unexpected Turns

Darling let's be honest; life throws us some curveballs. You might encounter criticism, even doubt, along this path. Guess what? That's fine! There are opportunities to reassess, reevaluate, and emerge stronger. A true Femme Fatale isn't immune to challenges; she rises above them.

Experiment and Adjust; Life is Your Laboratory.

As you embark on this transformative journey view your life as a space. Explore ways of expressing your Femme Fatale energy and be open to feedback from both you and others. Remember, this journey is not fixed; you're constantly evolving!

Taking Control of Your Story; Craft Your Narrative This is where the true power of developing your brand comes circle. It means recognizing and embracing your past and present while also taking control of your future by crafting it yourself. Don't allow society or anyone else to dictate who you should become. The Femme Fatale is more than a character in her story; she is an author who shapes her narrative.

There have it, my dear! Becoming the woman, you were destined to be is not a destination but an ongoing journey. Let me assure you it will be the adventure of your life. The world doesn't just need women; it needs awakened, empowered, and yes distinctly feminine women like yourself. You are now one of them. Step out into the world and let your captivating light shine even if others may not yet be ready for it – that's their concern, not yours.

Continue to radiate and grow your Femme Fatale!

CREATING A LIFE THAT HONORS YOUR DARK ENERGY; YOUR BLUEPRINT FOR A LIFE THAT'S AS ENIGMATIC AS YOU ARE

Hello there soul! So much has transpired between us on this journey together, hasn't it? From understanding the foundations of energy to fully embracing the essence of being a Femme Fatale, within yourself – we've experienced quite the rollercoaster ride.

Alright, let's bring everything together and delve into the art of creating a life that truly embraces your energy. This is the masterpiece, my dear!

Your Life, Your Way; The Empowering Force of Personal Freedom

First and foremost, remember that your life should be your domain and you are the reigning queen. What does this entail? It means you have the power to make decisions that align with your essence. From choosing the company you keep to welcoming energies into your space prioritize choices that resonate with your nature. Sovereignty isn't, about controlling others; it's about taking charge of your journey. Remember, you're the enchanting Femme Fatale shaping her narrative.

Creating a Sacred Haven in Your Environment

Let's focus on the surroundings for a moment. Your physical space mirrors your world. To honor and embrace your energy it's essential to cultivate an environment that serves as a sanctuary for recharging, rejuvenating, and tapping into the depths within you. Think of textures ambient lighting that exudes moodiness or even setting up an altar where you can engage in spiritual rituals. Transform your space into a temple celebrating every facet of your feminine essence.

Ambition; Unleashing the Femme Fatale, in Professional Settings

Who says you can't infuse elements of your energy into the professional realm? The qualities of a Femme Fatale, such, as confidence, allure, and wisdom hold value in aspects of life including a business setting. Whether you're leading a team or negotiating a contract you can utilize your energy to influence outcomes and create a fulfilling life that aligns with your ambitions. Let's break those barriers and reach heights together!

Building connections goes beyond mastering the art of seduction. To cultivate relationships that embrace your energy prioritize depth over surface-level interactions. Seek partnerships that nourish your soul and push you to grow. It's time to stop settling for anything other than what you deserve! Your feminine energy naturally attracts connections; use this power wisely.

Embracing your energy means embracing your capacity for continuous personal growth. Never stop learning. Whether through practice acquiring skills or focusing on self-improvement. Immerse yourself in books, workshops, or experiences that expand your understanding of both you and the world around you. Keep that energy flowing and evolving!

Remember; Your dark energy holds transformative potential not for yourself but for those, around you.

How can you use your influence to make an impact, on the world? Maybe it's through acts or simply by spreading love and wisdom in your community. Being a Femme Fatale means you have the power to make a difference; it's important to use that power.

What an incredible journey isn't it? Creating a life that embraces your energy is like crafting a masterpiece; it's something that takes dedication throughout your lifetime. The key is to be intentional with every action you take and every decision you make. You're not just living life; you're composing a story of a mysterious, powerful, and captivating Femme Fatale who radiates darkness.

I must say, I couldn't be prouder of you. Keep shining keep growing and above all continue embracing that intense energy within you.

CONCLUSION

MOVING FORWARD ON YOUR JOURNEY WHILE EMBRACING YOUR DARK FEMININE ENERGY

The Page but Not the Final Chapter!

You've absorbed the words embraced the wisdom and unraveled the secrets within these pages... Let me tell you something—this is far from being the end. No, my friend, this is merely the beginning of something fueled by your dark feminine energy. Consider this book as your ticket granting VIP access, to a realm filled with power, allure, and magnetic charm.

Get ready because your adventure is just starting!

Don't forget the four Ss, allure, confidentiality, tactics, and spirituality.

As you move forward always keep in mind these four Ss that form the foundation of your power. Whether you're navigating through office politics or captivating the man of your dreams these elements are your go-to tools. You'll use them like an enchantress concocting the perfect solution, for any challenge life throws at you.

The Seductive Woman in a Paced World

We live in an era where everything's fleeting – stories vanish posts get buried and attention spans are shorter than a TikTok video... You? You are timeless. The wisdom and strategies you've gained here are your armor in a world that constantly updates itself. While others fade away you will endure because you hold onto secrets that never lose their charm.

The Book Closes, The Legend Unfolds

Sure this book may be reaching its pages. Who says it's the end? It marks the beginning of your legacy. Years, from now people will still talk about that woman who entered a room and captivated the world with her presence.

That's who you are. You're not someone who reads about history; you're someone who makes history happen.

"It's Not Me It's My Energy" Embrace It

When things start going for you when people start being captivated by your charm it's tempting to think, "Wow maybe it's luck.". Don't believe that! It's not luck; it's the power of your energy, at work. Embrace it utilize it and direct it with purpose.

Cheers to a Lifetime of Embracing Your Femme Fatale Power!

You can close this book now. Don't forget what you've learned. Being a femme fatale is more than an action; it's a way of life. So, here's to you—may your feminine energy light up your path in the darkest times. May it guide those lost in the routine of life… Above all else may it bring you the fulfillment, influence, and profound happiness that you truly deserve.

So, my powerful femme fatale friend, are you ready to finish this chapter and embark on a journey, in your life? Because the world might not be prepared for what lies with you leading the way —. That's their concern to handle, not yours. Your mission? Tap into your power and allow others to witness both your strengths and vulnerabilities.

Until we cross paths again keep in mind that you're not simply living your life; you're crafting a captivating story. Write it skillfully. Future generations will cherish it.

This marks the conclusion of one chapter. The start of a tale that defines you.

Farewell, for now. Remember, in your exploration of the depths of energy there are no farewells—only fresh starts.

ACKNOWLEDGMENTS

Dear Cherished Reader,

Thank you so much for taking the time to explore "Dark Feminine Energy." I sincerely hope that your journey through its pages has been as transformative for you as it was for me in writing it.

If this book has stirred your spirit, I warmly invite you to share your reflections in a review. Your words carry the incredible power to illuminate and empower other women on their own paths to self-discovery, echoing a message of solidarity and strength that we all hold dear.

Your feedback is invaluable—not just as guidance for fellow readers, but as a vital contribution to this work's ongoing life and reach. It is a heartfelt act of support that can resonate with women across the world, potentially sparking transformative journeys for many.

With heartfelt gratitude for your time and your voice,

Nora Haze

Printed in Great Britain
by Amazon

44989450R00059